ARAM AND ISRAEL

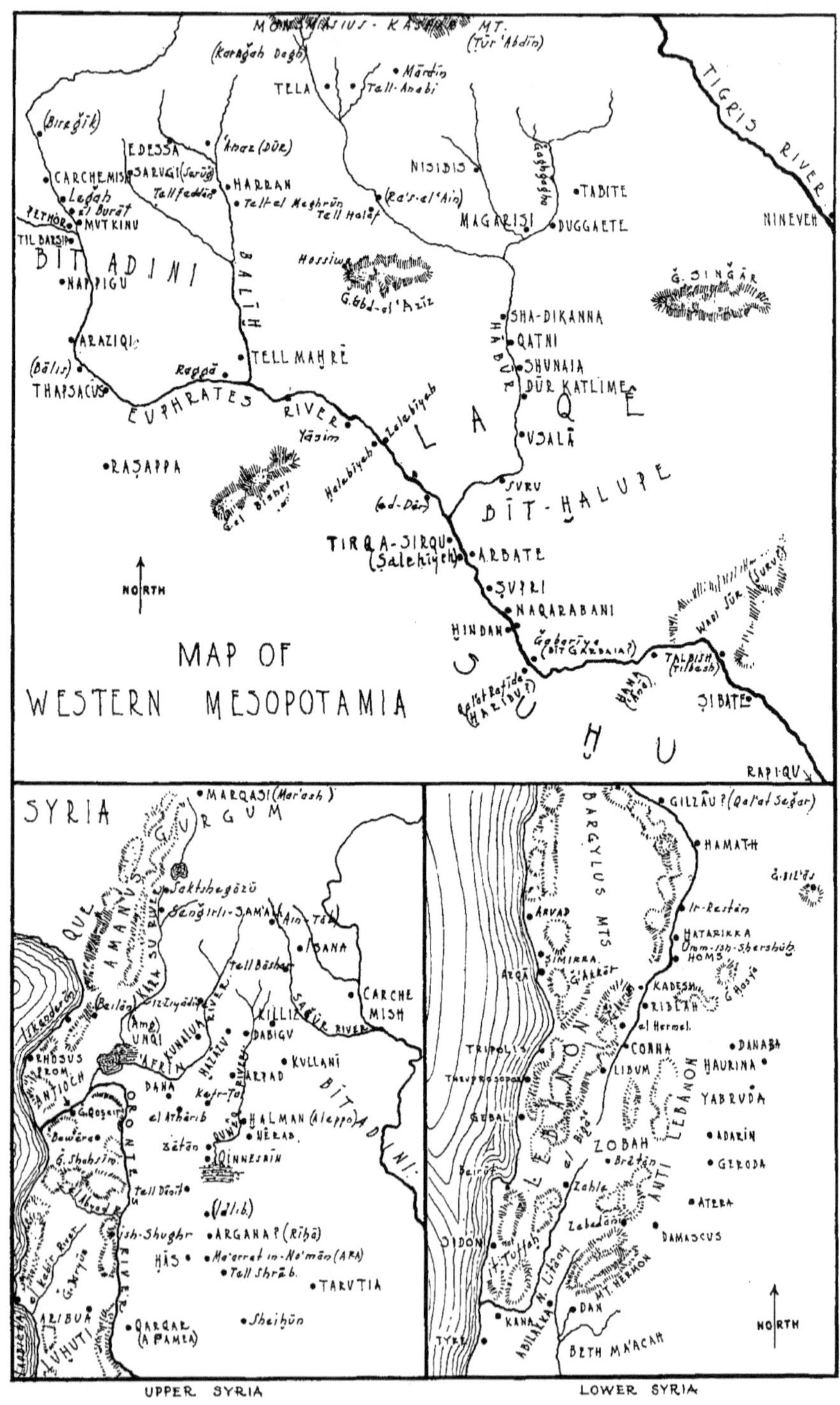

UPPER SYRIA

LOWER SYRIA

ARAM AND ISRAEL

OR

THE ARAMAEANS IN SYRIA AND MESOPOTAMIA

BY

EMIL G. H. KRAELING, Ph.D.

WIPF & STOCK · Eugene, Oregon

Wipf and Stock Publishers
199 W 8th Ave, Suite 3
Eugene, OR 97401

Aram and Israel
The Aramaeans in Syria and Mesopotamia
By Kraeling, Emil G. H.
ISBN 13: 978-1-60608-394-9
Publication date 01/07/2009
Previously published by Columbia University Press, 1918

NOTE

Gradually the tangled skein of the early history of Western Asia is being unwound. Through excavations on the one hand and intensive study of the received documents on the other, the relation is being understood born by the various peoples and races to one another; and light is being thrown upon the forces that played in the great historic drama that history has unrolled for us in this part of the world. Our own interest in this history is certain; for whatsoever we are and whatsoever we possess comes to us from the Eastern half of the Mediterranean Sea. The Coast and the Hinterland of that Sea have played a preponderating part in determining the influence that was supreme there.

One of the peoples engaged in playing that part were the Aramaeans. Who they were and what their rôle was have been studied by Dr. Kraeling with much assiduity and with great care. From the various quarters he has gathered every scintilla of evidence available; and, in the following pages, he has put this evidence into connected form, so that he who reads may learn. It is with much pleasure that I commend the work that Dr. Kraeling has done.

RICHARD GOTTHEIL

Columbia University
Nov. 7, 1917

PARENTIBUS SUIS

PRIMIS ET OPTIMIS PRAECEPTORUM

HUNC LIBRUM

DEDICAT AUCTOR

FOREWORD

THE following pages purport only to give a sketch of the history of those Aramaean groups, which are of interest to the student of the Old Testament. I have endeavored to make my account readable and yet thoroughly scientific. The book offers no new and astonishing revelations, but I hope that here and there scholars may find a modest wayside flower worth the picking. The original sources are constantly cited. The secondary sources, so far as they were of value to me, or may be to the reader, are also continually referred to. The inclusion of numerous references in the text has made many abbreviations necessary and has caused the omission of the names of authors of magazine articles quoted. Only those versed in Oriental studies will realize how much we owe to men like Delitzsch, Hommel, Johns, Kittel, Lidzbarski, Meyer, Müller, Sachau, Schiffer, Streck, Winckler and others, whose researches have clarified the history of the ancient east and many obscure passages in the inscriptions. I have devoted special attention to geographical matters, for geography forms the basis of exact historical study. The transcription of modern place names generally follows that of Richard Kiepert.

I cannot close without expressing my deepest gratitude to Professors Richard Gottheil and J. Dynely Prince of Columbia for the kindness they have shown me, as well as to Professors A. T. Clay of Yale, J. A. Montgomery of Pennsylvania, and to Professors F. Weissbach, Geheimrat H. Zimmern, Geheimrat D. R. Kittel of Leipzig, my revered guides in the realm of Oriental research.

EMIL G. H. KRAELING

Luther's Birthday (Nov. 10), 1917

CONTENTS

INTRODUCTION

The Sources

CHAPTER I

The Geographical Background

CHAPTER II

The Aramaean Migration

CHAPTER III

The Aramaeans of Harran

CHAPTER IV

The Invasion of Palestine

CHAPTER V

The Rise of the Aramaeans in Central Syria

CHAPTER VI

The Early Kings of Damascus

CHAPTER VII

The Mesopotamian Kingdoms

CHAPTER VIII

The North Syrian States

CHAPTER IX

The Supremacy of Damascus

CHAPTER XIV

Kings of Sam'al

CHAPTER XV

The Last Rebellions

LIST OF ABBREVIATIONS

A A	F. Hommel. — Aufsätze und Abhandlungen. 1892 ff.
A B L	R. F. Harper. — Assyrian and Babylonian Letters. 1892 ff.
A D D	C. H. W. Johns. — Assyrian Deeds and Documents. Vols. II, III. 1901.
A E T	Herzfeld und Sarre. — Am Euphrat und Tigris. Vol. I. 1911.
A H T	F. Hommel. — The Ancient Hebrew Tradition. 1898.
A J S L	American Journal of Semitic Languages.
A K A	King and Budge. — Annals of the Kings of Assyria. Vol. I. 1902.
A O F	H. Winckler. — Altorientalische Forschungen. 1897 f.
A S	Ausgrabungen in Sendschirli. Pts 1–4. 1893–1911.
A T V	H. Winckler. — Alttestamentliche Untersuchungen. 1892.
B A	Beiträge zur Assyriologie. Ed. Delitzsch and Haupt. 1881 f.
B A R	J. H. Breasted. — Ancient Records of Egypt. 5 vols. 1896 ff.
Böhl	F. Böhl. — Kanaanäer und Hebräer. 1911.
C I S	Corpus Inscriptionum Semiticarum. Part II.
Clay	A. T. Clay. — Amurru the Home of the Northern Semites. 1909.
C T	Cuneiform Texts from Babylonian Tablets. 1896 f.
D P	Fr. Delitzsch. — Wo lag das Paradies? 1881.
E K	Carl Ritter. — Erdkunde, XV, XVII. 1854.
E S E	M. Lidzbarski. — Ephemeris für Semitische Epigraphik. 1900 ff.
G A	Ed. Meyer. — Geschichte des Altertums. I, pt. 2. 1908.
G G	F. Hommel. — Geographie und Geschichte des Alten Orient. 1907.
G V J	R. Kittel. — Geschichte des Volkes Israel. 1909 f.
H C	C. H. W. Johns. — Assyrian Doomsday Book. 1901.
J B L	Journal of Biblical Literature.
K A T	Winckler und Zimmern. — Die Keilinschriften und das Alte Testament. 3. Aufl. 1902.
K H K	Kurzer Hand. — Kommentar zum Alten Testament (edited by Karl Marti): Budde. — Samuelis. 1897; Benzinger. — Könige. 1899.
Kn	Knudzton. — Die Tontafeln von El-Amarna. 1907 f.
LXX	The Greek Septuagint Version of the Old Testament.
M A E	W. M. Müller. — Asien und Europa. 1893.
Masp III	G. Maspero. — Passing of Empires. 1900.
M D O G	Mitteilungen der Deutschen Orient Gesellschaft.

LIST OF ABBREVIATIONS

M K A	L. Messerschmidt. — Keilschrifttexte aus Assur Historischen Inhalts. 1911.
M T	The Massoretic Text of the Old Testament.
M V A G	Mitteilungen der Vorderasiatischen Gesellschaft.
N S I	G. A. Cooke. — North Semitic Inscriptions. 1903.
O L Z	Orientalistische Literaturzeitung.
Procksch	Die Genesis. 1913.
P S B A	Proceedings of the Society of Biblical Archaeology.
R	H. Rawlinson. — Cuneiform Inscriptions of Western Asia. 5 vols. 1861 f.
R A	Revue Archéologique.
R T P	H. Rost. — Keilschrifttexte Tiglathpileser's III. 1893.
S A	S. Schiffer. — Die Aramäer. Geographisch-Historische Untersuchungen. 1911.
Sachau	Ed. Sachau. — Reise in Syrien und Mesopotamien. 1883.
S B A	Sitzungsberichte der Berliner Akademie der Wissenschaften.
Textb.	H. Winckler. — Keilinschriftliches Textbuch zum Alten Testament. 3d ed. 1908.
W G I	H. Winckler. — Geschichte Israels. 2 vols. 1895, 1900.
Z A	Zeitschrift für Assyriologie.
Z A W	Zeitschrift für Alttestamentliche Wissenschaft.
Z D M G	Zeitschrift der Deutschen Morgenländischen Gesellschaft.
Z D P V	Zeitschrift des Deutschen Palästina Vereins.

THE ARAMAEANS
IN
SYRIA AND MESOPOTAMIA

INTRODUCTION

THE SOURCES

As the early history of mankind is unrolled before our eyes and as we learn of the struggles of nations whose names have been forgotten for ages, we must needs marvel over nature's endless capacity for producing ever new variations of the race, with a Babel of tongues so vast and bewildering. Yet, somehow, each of these peoples that once trod over the face of the globe had its place in the structure of progress and contributed some new energy toward the onward march of the world. The doctrine that it is not the nature of the absolute to reveal itself fully in one individual, may well be applied to the peoples of the earth. None of them alone represents the ideal of humanity, but each possesses something which it must give toward the realization of this ideal before it vanishes to be no more seen. And in this great fellowship Aram, too, has its place. True, its mission was not to create eternal values, as is the case with Hellas and Israel. It was rather the predestined medium through which these values were to be communicated throughout the Orient.

The history of the Aramaeans cannot yet be written. Through the gloom that enshrouds their destinies our sources only now and then cast a fitful glimmer. We possess merely flash-light pictures, taken here and there, and preserved in papyri or engraved on stone or written on clay. These the chronicler must piece together; they must speak to him and reveal the heart-beats of the race and enable him to paint his *sujet* in colors true to life. Of the Aramaeans we know just enough to give an impressionistic design of who they were and what befell them.

Only a few original documents of old Aramaean origin have come down to us. The numerous Aramaic inscriptions of Nabataean and Palmyrene provenance,[1] the valuable Papyri from the upper Nile, dating from the Persian era,[2] do not concern us here; for the period with which we propose to deal is the one marked by the hegemony of Assyria, which ended with the fall of Nineveh 606 B.C. The old Aramaic inscriptions antedating this event all come from northern and central Syria. Foremost among them are the inscriptions of the kings of Sam'al, Kilammu (who, though an Aramaean, still writes in Phoenician), Panammu and Bar-Rekab, belonging to the eighth century and unearthed at Senğirli, at the foot of the Amanus range (Chs. X, XIV). Of equal importance is also the stele of Zakir, king of Hamath on the Orontes, from the same period (Ch. XI). These are sources of the very first rank and offer valuable insight into the language, life and religion of the inhabitants of Syria.[3]

Our chief geographical and historical information, however, is gained from contemporaneous records in other tongues. The Egyptian monuments, though of great value for previous Syrian history, furnish only small gleanings for the Aramaean epoch.[4] The Hittite inscriptions, from Carchemish, Mar'ash, Hamath and elsewhere, will doubtless become an important source for

[1] Cf. the Corpus Inscriptionum Semiticarum, T. II, Pt. 1; also Lidzbarski, Nordsemitische Epigraphik, 1898, and the English translations with commentary in Cooke, North Semitic Inscriptions, 1903.

[2] Sayce and Cowley, The Assuan Papyri, 1907; Sachau, Aramäische Papyrus und Ostraka aus Elephantine, 1911.

[3] The mortuary inscriptions of the priests Sin-zir-ban and Agbar of Nêrab date probably from 605–552 B.C. (N S I 187).

[4] Cf. Breasted, Ancient Records of Egypt, 5 vols., 1896 f., and especially W. M. Müller, Asien und Europa, 1893.

our knowledge when once they can be made to yield their time-honored secrets.[1] But at present we must mainly depend upon the cuneiform literature of Babylonia and Assyria. The dawn of Aramaean history greets us, it seems, in archaic inscriptions from Nippur and Lagash from the third millennium B.C.[2] The wanderings of the Aramaeans may then be traced in letters of the Hammurapi dynasty[3] and of the Amarna age,[4] and more clearly in recently discovered monuments of the early Assyrian kings Adadnirâri I and Shalmaneser I,[5] as well as in the Prism of Tiglathpileser I and in the so-called "Broken Obelisk."[6] (Ch. II) From the tenth century on we learn of Aramaean kingdoms in Mesopotamia and Syria. For our knowledge of Mesopotamian geography the Annals of Tukulti-Ninib[7] form a welcome addition to the inscriptions of Ashurnazirpal[8] and Shalmaneser III.[9] The two last named monarchs, together with Tiglathpileser IV,[10] are our main source for the history and geography of the Aramaean states in Syria. Nor should we omit the mention of Adadnirâri IV[11] and of Sargon.[12] In some instances the Assyrian Eponym Canon,[13] so invaluable for our chronology, furnishes brief but precious data. In studying the Assyrian annals we must everywhere bear in mind the fact that they are prone to

[1] Cf. the account of Garstang, Land of the Hittites, 1910.

[2] Cf. Thureau-Dangin, Die Sumerischen und Akkadischen Königsinschriften, 1907.

[3] Cf. Ungnad, Altbabylonische Briefe aus der Hammurapi Zeit, '13.

[4] Cf. Knudtzon, Die El-Amarna Tafeln, 2 vols., 1911f.; also the Boghaz-Koi Archives, cited by Winckler in 'Vorläufige Nachrichten,' M D O G '07 no. 35.

[5] Collected in Messerschmidt, Keilschrifttexte aus Assur historischen Inhalts, 1911.

[6] Now newly edited by King and Budge, The Annals of the Kings of Assyria, Vol. I, 1902, p. 128 f.

[7] Scheil, Annales de Tukulti-Ninip II, '09.

[8] Newly edited, A K A p. 155 ff.

[9] For the present we must depend on Schrader's Keilinschriftliche Bibliothek, I, '89, p. 129 ff.

[10] The final edition is that of Rost, Keilschrifttexte Tiglathpilesers 1893.

[11] Cf. Keilinschriftliche Bibliothek, I, p. 188 f.

[12] The final edition is that of Winckler, Keilschrifttexte Sargons, 1889.

[13] Cf. Keilinschriftliche Bibliothek, I, 208 f.; Textb., 73 f.

exaggerate greatly to the glory of their authors, and to omit all mention of reverses. Sometimes, too, the order of events is logical rather than chronological, and occasionally important discrepancies appear in the various inscriptions of the same king. Here the sound methods of historical research must be applied to obtain the truth.[1] From the cultural and religious standpoint the Harran Census[2] (Ch. III), the Mesopotamian contract literature[3] and the treaty of Ashur-nirâri with Mati-ilu of Arpad (Ch. XII) are extremely illuminating. For the life in the provinces and subjected Aramaean principalities the letters of the Sargonid period offer meager information.[4].

Our next great source is the Old Testament. True, the historical reminiscences concerning Aram's relations to Israel preserved in this great treasury of ancient lore are seldom contemporaneous. Most of the documents are indeed quite far removed from the happenings that they narrate. Here the work of a generation of scholars enables us to differentiate between various oral and written sources, with their diverging traditions, which the sacred writers employed.[5] The exact nature of events, consequently, cannot always be fully determined. But where the account, on internal evidence, can be shown to be close in point of time to the events related, the standard of accuracy is usually very great. For the writers of Hebrew history were not, like the Assyrian scribes, official chroniclers bent on glorifying their sovereigns; they did not shrink from describing disasters and defeats. On the other hand, however, their religious bias often, as in the case of Ahab, prevented them from giving a correct estimate of personalities.

[1] An auspicious beginning in exact critical study has been made by Olmstead, Assyrian Historiography, 1914.

[2] Johns, Assyrian Doomsday Book or Liberal Census of the District round Harran, 1901.

[3] Johns, Assyrian Deeds and Documents, 3 vols., 1898–1901.

[4] Cf. Harper's great corpus Assyrian and Babylonian Letters, 14 vols., 1892 f.

[5] Cf. above all Rudolf Kittel's Geschichte des Volkes Israel, 2 vols., 1909 f., with its detailed treatment of the sources.

For the early period of Aramaean history the Old Testament traditions must be used with the greatest of care. It should always be borne in mind that the Hebrew writers did not aspire to set forth the history of the heathen peoples round about. Where they refer to them it is merely a matter of accident. And then the accuracy of their information needs to be closely examined. No scholar would therefore presume to make these traditions the basis of a history. On the other hand we may thankfully make use of them, at least by way of illustration, where they harmonize with what we learn from the monuments. It will be seen that in a surprising number of instances the true course of events is mirrored in the Old Testament. Thus the patriarchal period, beneath the guise of personal adventure, reflects the Aramaean migration and even the social life of certain tribes (cf. below Chs. II–IV). The period of the Judges has only vague news to offer, and under the first kings of Israel we do not fare much better, but nevertheless we shall find certain fixed points of tradition which we can safely adopt for the reconstruction of Aramaean history (Ch. V). From the time of Omri on, however, we are better informed and occasionally have excellent contemporary witnesses of events. It is unnecessary to deal in further detail with individual passages here. The use that is made of them in the course of our narrative will indicate sufficiently to those versed in critical problems what attitude is assumed towards them in each instance. Nowhere is a light-hearted acceptance of mere tradition to be found, as little as an espousal of the fanciful theories of some moderns.

The authors of the Graeco-Roman world have little to offer for our theme. Perhaps the Eremboi of the Odyssey (4, 84), to whom Menelaus came after visiting Ethiopians and Sidonians, or the Arimoi of the Iliad (2, 782), in whose land the monster Typhon was concealed, may represent our Aramaeans, for it is not at all unlikely that the echo of the gigantic Aramaean onset should have reached the ears of the Homeric bards on the shores of Hellas. At the time of Herodotus and Xenophon, however, the

Aramaean wave had long spent its force and the western Aramaean states had crumbled, so that we learn nothing of value for our purpose from their pages. If Josephus (Ant. VII, 5, 2) cites for the history of Aram the works of Nicolaus of Damascus, the contents of the quotation cannot impress us, for they offer merely misunderstandings spun out of the biblical traditions.[1] Only for the reconstruction of ancient geography [2] can we gain information of value from Greek and Latin authors, and perhaps also for our knowledge of the Aramaean religion,[3] though the task here becomes extremely difficult in view of the syncretism prevalent in Syria in such matters since early days.

These then are the materials out of which the workman with keen chisel must carve the history of the Aramaean neighbors of Israel.

[1] Cf. Schrader's Keilinschriften und Geschichtsforschung, '78, 379 f.

[2] Cf. especially the great work of Carl Ritter, Erdkunde, Vols. XV and XVII. The results of modern travel and of classical geography are presented in the invaluable maps of Syria and Mesopotamia by Richard Kiepert, appended to von Oppenheim's, Vom Mittelmeer zum Persischen Golf, 2 vols., 1899–1900.

[3] Lucian's De Dea Syria dealing with the worship of Atargatis at Hierapolis, the ancient Aramaean Nappigu, is the most noteworthy classical contribution.

CHAPTER I

THE GEOGRAPHICAL BACKGROUND

In order to understand properly the history of any people, it is first necessary to portray the setting upon which it transpired. For by the physiography of the land, its position in respect to other portions of the earth's surface, its natural barriers and features, the destiny of its inhabitants is largely controlled. The scene of Aramaean history, so far as it is the object of the present study, is laid chiefly in Syria and in the great river country east of it, in Mesopotamia.

These two regions in reality form a unit, for the Euphrates, which is supposed to mark their boundary, cannot be regarded as a barrier of importance. In reality Syria extends as far east as Nisibis and the valley of the Ḫābūr, and "Mesopotamia" should be applied only to that part of the Ǧezireh between the Ḫābūr and Babylonia (G A § 332). Thus from the viewpoint of the geographer the northern border of "Greater Syria" should be drawn over the Tūr ʻAbdīn and Karağah Dagh to Samosata and Marʻash. For practical reasons, however, we shall do well to abide by the traditional terminology and to deal with western Mesopotamia as distinct from Syria.

Two streams, both tributary to the Euphrates, divide western Mesopotamia vertically. From the highlands on both sides of the Nimrūd Dagh near Edessa the Balīḫ originates and flows down to meet the great river near Raqqā. The original capital of the Balīḫ valley is Harran whose importance, however, was later overshadowed by Urhai (Edessa) from which this district received the name Osroene. Further east a larger stream, the Ḫābūr, descends from the Karağah Dagh and Tūr ʻAbdīn and merges into the Euphrates near ed-Dēr. Along its course numerous important cities flourished, in the north notably Mardin and Nisibis.

Syria west of the Euphrates was for ages known as Amurrû. Originally this term pertained only to a powerful state whose center was in the Lebanon district. This is attested to by the fact that the region at the passes of the Amanus is called Sam'al or "north," while Yamîn or "south" (later Yemen) clings to the district south of Palestine. (K A T 18) Such a terminology can only have arisen when the center of gravity, politically speaking, was midway between Gaza and the Cilician Gate, i.e., in central Syria. The Akkadians however called the entire west-land Amurrû as *pars pro toto,* although traces of the older usage are by no means infrequent.

A glance at the map reveals the unique position held by Syria as the bridge between Eurasia and Africa. The arid and inhospitable nature of Arabia forces all those who would travel from one continent to the other to traverse this narrow strip of land along the Mediterranean coast. Moreover, the existence of advanced civilizations on the Nile and Euphrates, each with commodities desirable for the other, created an impetus for traffic. Over the great caravan road from Egypt to Gaza, Megiddo, Damascus and Aleppo, and thence to Mesopotamia or to Asia Minor rolled much of the wealth of the ancient world.

A nation situated on such a great thoroughfare should be a world power. This was indeed realized in very early days by the state of Amurrû, which together with Elam, Subartu and Akkad made up the four points of the compass, as being the most important states in their quarter (B A VI 17). But with the rise of imperialism in Egypt and in Mesopotamia the power of the Syrian empire was doomed. For its borders lay open towards both of its great neighbors. And the billows of migrating peoples that descended from Asia Minor and Armenia, and issued out of Arabia were destined to strike Syria with irresistible impact.

The natural features of the land predestined it to the fate of producing a number of small rival states. For it divides into three latitudinal zones. Each of these is marked by rivers. The southern zone is watered by the Jordan, which rises from the foothills of Mt. Hermon and flows south into the Dead Sea. Within this region the Philistaean plain and the hill country of Judah and of Ephraim are the main features. The central zone is marked by the Orontes, which flows north between the Lebanon and Antilebanon and around the Bargylus in a large loop to the Mediterranean. Between these two zones lies the *Biqâ'*, a fertile plain between the Lebanon and Antilebanon, forming the "Coele" or "belly" of Syria. The coastal plain of central Syria is narrow and intermittent, and isolated from the rest of the land by the steep walls of the Lebanon; protected situation and splendid harbors have made this strip a distinct country, Phoenicia. The northern zone is marked by the twin rivers, Afrīn and Kara-Su. The Amanus mountains and the highlands east to 'Aintab form the watershed from which these latter streams flow south to the lake of Antioch and thence with the Orontes to the sea. (E K XV[1] 20) It is immediately apparent that the southern sector will lie chiefly within the sphere of Egypt's influence, while the northern sector will be controlled by the cultural forces of Mesopotamia and Asia Minor. Only in the central portion of the land will an independent life be at all possible.

Coelesyria, the biblical Aram, it indeed seems, has been especially favored by nature to fulfill a historical though limited task. Its heart is the Marsyas plain (il Biqâ'), a beautiful garden spot watered by the Litâny river, and protected on all sides by the ramparts of great mountains. Through it leads the main caravan road of Syria. But there is also a second highway, which in a large loop circumvents the Biqâ' and passes through Damascus, an oasis on the edge of the desert. Whether the Biqâ' or Damascus becomes the center of a possible kingdom, a conflict with their southerly neighbor is inevitable. For the first goal of a rising nation must be to gain an open road to the sea, and this road nature marked out through northern Palestine to Akko. (G V J II 323). To safeguard the kingdom the region of Gilead must also be annexed, since it forms a dangerous salient on the left flank. The struggle between Aram and Israel is therefore a logical necessity.

As for the remainder of the land, our superficial survey of its topography gives us an indication of where states of any size might spring up. In the south the districts of Idumaea, Judaea and Ephraim as well as the Shephelah plains furnish opportunity for principalities to crystallize. In the central portion, the Lebanon district, just described, and the Bargylus district from the Tripolis to the Laodicea highways are apparent foci. At the dividing line of the central and the northern sector the lake of Antioch with the fertile ʿAmq will see the rise of a power controlling the road to the gulf of Alexandrette, as well as the mountain district between the Orontes and the way to Laodicea. Above this the plain at the headwaters of the Kara-Su east of the important Amanus passes will be a center for the Amanus region. On the eastern side of the northern sector there will be a few petty principalities in the sphere of the Chalus and Sağūr rivers. On the Euphrates river the point where navigation begins, near Ğerabis, and the great caravan-crossing at the mouth of the Sağūr are likely to be the centers of strong political units which will share the control of the western Osroene with Harran.

The history of the Aramaeans, in these regions chiefly, will be followed in the subsequent chapters. The principalities outside of this sphere inhabited by Aramaeans will only be touched on in passing. We are not writing a history of the Aramaean race. We are merely giving an account of the fate of the Aramaeans, so far as it is entwined with the destiny of the "chosen people."

CHAPTER II

THE ARAMAEAN MIGRATION

FROM the vast, little explored land of Arabia have come the various migrations of Semitic peoples by which the more fertile regions to the north and west have been overrun in different epochs. All attempts at locating the Semitic cradle in Armenia fail because of the presence there of Turanian races in extremely early days; for the original habitat of Semite and Turanian must have lain far apart. The ultimate home of the Semites may have been in Abessynia or elsewhere; but most certainly Arabia was an important center for the race and the starting point of its migrations so far as they lie in the clear light of history.

The earliest Semitic migration is the Akkadian (Semitic-Babylonian), which began in the fourth or fifth millennium B.C. The Akkadian language stands apart from the other Semitic languages, which have less in common with it than with each other, so that it was the first to branch out from the common tree. The Akkadian migration is shrouded in the mists of the past. When history begins we see the Akkadians building their state in northern Irak and battling with the Sumerians in the south.

Soon after, in the third millennium B.C., the Gezireh must have been overrun by Hittite peoples from Asia Minor, for the oldest known rulers of Nineveh, who reigned before the first dynasty of Babylon, Aushpia and Kikia, are of this Turanian stock (B A VII 5, 8). Furthermore, we find opposite the Ḫābūr's mouth a city of Tirqa, the name of which immediately reminds of the Hittite deity Tarqu, and a state called Ḫana, which has its counterpart in the Ḫani, Yaḫan and Ḫanigalbat in northern Syria and Armenia, so that we are tempted to see in it a deposit of the Hittite migration that came from these quarters. Indeed

"Ḫatti" appears to be only a feminine form of "Ḫana" (D P 170). The names of the cities Zakku-Isharlim and Zakku-Igitlim, appearing in one of the Ḫana Tablets,[1] also seem to be Hittite (G G 50), and the same is true of the deity Idurmer[2] that occurs in an oath formula alongside of Shamash and Dagan. Below Ḫana on the Euphrates lay the regions of Suḫu[3] and Mari.[4] Perhaps we may find here also a slight trace of the Hittite invasion in the name of the god Yabliya mentioned in an Old Babylonian letter dealing with happenings in this region.[5]

Upon the heels of this Hittite movement must have come the Amorite migration. The original home of this people was South Arabia, for its religious concepts and expressions as evidenced by the personal names are startlingly similar to those of the later Minaeans and Sabaeans (A H T 83 f.). They first invaded Syria and established there the great state of Amurrû even before the Akkadians completely gained control of Babylonia. It may be assumed that the Amorites came from the Ḥiǧāz, for the old highway of the gold and frankinscense merchants traversed this region of the Red Sea coast. In the country east of the Jordan,

[1] Cf. P S B A '07: 180. Since Tell ʿIshar between ed-Dēr and Ṣāleḥīye seems to be the place where these tablets were found, the Tell must cover the remains of the city of Tirqa, the capital of Ḫana. The latter name has also survived in the modern ʿAna (Anatho) further down the river.

[2] Clay, Miscellaneous Inscriptions, '16: 3, however, would make this deity Amoritish, a variant of Amar.

[3] A most interesting inscription from this region, belonging, however, to a much later period, is that of Shamash-resh-uṣur, governor of Suḫi and Mari (Weissbach, Babylonische Miszellen, '03, p. 9 ff.). It recounts an attack by hostile neighbors, the Aramaean Tu'mânu, who are partly killed, partly subjugated; then it describes the restoration of the canal of Suḫi and a boat-ride upon the same. After this it tells of the planting of date palms and the erection of the throne in Ribanish, and finally of the building of the city Gabbaribanî. Other cities mentioned are Ḫarze, Yâbi, Railu, Kar-Nabu Yaduru and Ukulai. — Suḫu is probably the Shuach of Gen. 25: 2. Cf. Job 2: 11, 8: 1, 25: 1, 42: 9. Cf. also Delitzsch, Hiob, '02, p. 139.

[4] Clay, Miscellaneous Inscriptions, p. 4, identifies Mari with the Merra of Isidore of Charax, which must be sought at El Irzi.

[5] Ungnad, Babylonische Briefe aus der Hammurapizeit, '13, no. 238; also M V A G '01: 144.

place names like Mefa'at, Sebam, Dibon, Yashimoth, Ma'on, which occur also in the South Arabian regions of Hadramaut, Saba and Ma'in, show the path taken by the Amorites.[1] From Syria they gradually moved westward down the Euphrates. Especially the regions of Ḫana, Suḫu and Mari were centers of Amorite life and religion, notably of the Dagan cult. From these regions the attacks of the Amorites must have been launched against Babylonia. Thus Ishbi-Urra, founder of the Isin Dynasty, is called "Man of Mari." The kings of the first dynasty of Babylon from Sumu-abu to Samsuditana are all Amorites, as their names reveal. The greatest of them was Hammurapi[2] who even called himself king of Amurrû. Wherever these Amorites went they took with them their summus deus Amar, from whom they proudly derive their name, and other gods of their pantheon. (Clay 95f) They even founded a city of Amurrû near Sippar and in this locality were very numerous.[3]

The third great Semitic migration, the Aramaean, must have started from the highland region of the Neǧd in inner Arabia. From this fertile district three highways run in northeasterly direction. Two of these, the Wadi er-Rumma and the parallel, more southerly ed-Dawâsir, lead directly to Chaldaea; the former issues near the mouth of the great river, the latter opposite the island of Dilmun (Bahrein). A third road, the Wadi Sirhān (originating in the Hauran), led in antiquity from the Ǧōf, an oasis north of the Neǧd, to the vicinity of Basra (A A 331). Any Semitic migration from Arabia into the Euphrates valley must come by these three roads. In consequence, the Aramaeans ought first to appear in Chaldaea.

Now it is known that even before the Amorites from the west conquered Babylonia, there existed in the Chaldaean plains a population of nomadic Semites with whom the Sumero-Akkadians

[1] Cf. Grimme, Mohammed, p. 14 f.

[2] In the Ḫana texts the name of this king is written Ḫammurapiḫ. This leads me to conclude that the correct etymology is "'Amm (the moongod) is exalted," $\sqrt{\text{rafa'a}}$.

[3] Cf. Ranke, Personal Names of the Hammurabi Dynasty, '05, 34.

came into contact.[1] Hommel has shown from a large number of Arabic loan words and formations in the Akkadian language that these Chaldaean Semites were already present in very early days and has claimed that the later Aramaeans were their descendants. (G G 130f.) Especially the vicinity of Erech seems to have been infested by these Semitic tribes. Thus we know of a Sheikh Anam of the hordes of Erech, son of Bêl-shimea, named alongside of the king Sin-Gāmil, who restored the wall of Erech.[2] With this we must also combine the expression Uruk-supuri, "Erech of the sheepfolds," in the Gilgamesh-Epic (G G 361) and the tradition which makes Nimrod the Cushite (from South Arabia?) builder of Erech (Gen. 10:10). Furthermore we learn from the Urra myth of a people called the Suti [3] who bear some connection with the licentious cult of Ishtar at Erech (col. II 8). A still earlier reference, however, to these Suti occurs in a letter from the time of Hammurapi.[4] In this letter a trader, who has been imprisoned for embezzlement and who had been sent by his employer across the Euphrates with a shipment of oil, gives assurance of his innocence and places the blame upon the Suti who have attacked and robbed him. These Suti are therefore present in Shumer already in the days of the first dynasty. Indeed we may possibly trace them back to the time of the Dynasty of Ur, for Arad-Nannar of Lagash calls himself "ruler of the *Su* people." [5] From Shumer they migrated westward in the succeeding centuries, for the Amarna letters (ca. 1400 B.C.) show us the Suti present in Syria and opposite Mesopotamia. Thus the Assyrian king Ashur-uballit writes (Kn. no. 16:38f.) that the Suti have pursued and held up the messengers of the Egyptian monarch, but that he had rescued them. They are mentioned by Rib-Addi of Gebal in connection with warlike operations and occur even in the letters of Yitia of Ashkelon and Zimridi of Lachish

[1] Grimme, *l.c.*, p. 5.

[2] Thureau-Dangin, Königsinschriften, p. 223.

[3] The Suti are called ṣâb ṣêri, "warriors of the plains," IV R 44, 1, 20.

[4] C T II pl. 19; cf. Ungnad, Briefe aus der Zeit Hammurapis, no 154.

[5] Cf. Thureau-Dangin, Königsinschriften, '07, 149.

(cf. Kn. 45, 1038). A little later the Cassite Kadashman-ḫarbe tried to safeguard the road to Amurrû by digging wells and subjecting the Suti (A O F I 147). Another part of this people moved northward towards Bagdad rather than to Syria, and maintained themselves there until quite late, giving their name to the Sittacene of classical geography (K A T 22). From these indications we may conclude that the Suti originally tented in the desert from Erech to Babylon, — in other words, they belonged to the early Chaldaeans. It is impossible in consequence to reckon them to the Amorite group, since they must have come from the Wadi er-Rumma and the Wadi Sirḥān into Chaldaea. We must rather count them among the vanguard of the Aramaeans.[1] The worship of the deity Amurru, accredited to them in later times in an Assyrian god-list, they may have adopted in early days from the Amorites. Originally they must have been worshipers of Athtar, then of the Akkadian Ishtar.

In the O. T. the westward trend of the Suti may be reflected in the account of Terah's migration from Ur Kasdīm.[2] Abraham is not specifically called an Aramaean, though ethnically he belongs to this group. The same we have found to be true of the Suti. The O. T. narrator would perhaps reckon Terah's family to the Chaldaeans. By this latter term the Aramaean inhabitants of the lower Euphrates, the Kaldi, were designated from the ninth century B.C. on. The Hebrew term Kasdīm must have passed

[1] Troublesome is the problem of the relation of the Suti to the Guti. They appear often side by side in the inscriptions, and seem to be meant by the biblical Koa and Shoa (D P 225 ff.). The term Guti does not refer exclusively to the non-Semitic people of the northern mountains. Thus the Guti who plundered Sippar according to the inscription of Nabonidus (Const. IV 21) are the Aramaeans whom Erba Marduk repelled from Babylonia in the eighth century (Z A XXIII 218). And the biblical use of Koa must also have such nomadic Aramaeans in view (Ezech. 23: 23). We should therefore define the *Guti* as the partly Aramaean, originally perhaps purely Alarodian nomads east of the Tigris, and the *Suti* as the Semitic nomads west of the Tigris.

[2] This Ur can only refer to the great city of early Sumerian culture. It is unnecessary to suppose an Ur in Mesopotamia or to have recourse to the Amurru (= Uru) near Sippar (Clay 190), which was an Amorite center and not an Aramaean.

over into Palestinian tradition before this time, since it represents an older stage of the name (A H T 210). Kasdīm seems to be derived from the Babylonian "*kishadu*" or "shore." (G G 245) The form Kasdīyīm used by Ezechiel (23:14) is the most exact and must be the equivalent of *Kishadaeans or people from the shore of the Euphrates (or the sea). As we shall yet learn (Ch. IV), the name "Hebrew" attributed to Abraham is virtually synonymous in meaning. That the Aramaeans came from Chaldaea is the view also of Amos 9:7, "Have I not brought Israel out of Egypt, and the Philistine from Kaphtor and the Aramaeans from Qir?" Where is Qir? We are led by Is. 22:6, where it is brought into relation with Elam, to seek it in southern Babylonia.[1] If we dare place any reliance on 2 Kings 16: 9, which, it seems to me, is an intentional reference to Amos 1:5, we can recall the fact that Tiglathpileser actually did deport captives to the region of the lower Tigris (A T U 104, 178). Hommel was led to find Qir in Gir-su (G G 189), but whether the two elements of this name can be separated in this fashion remains problematic. It seems however, that Haupt has shown the way to the right solution of this question.[2] He points out that the modern name of Ur, "Muqayyar," means "asphalted or built with asphalt." The word Qir in Arabic means "pitch." In Hebrew, Qir means wall or city, but originally must have signified "built with asphalt." Now the Sumerian word for city is URU, which also means "foundation." Haupt therefore holds that Qir is a synonym of URU and may have been a by-name of Ur used perhaps by the Beduin of the region.[3] If this be true, as seems plausible, then the tradition of Amos vindicates Genesis 11:31.

[1] As A T V 178 proves, the text must be amended "Elam raises the quiver and Aram mounts the horse and Qir bares the shield." The preceding verse must be amended with Haupt (cf. note 13) into "Koa and Shoa batter against the mountain."

[2] In a paper entitled "Ur of the Chaldees" in the J B L Vol. XXXVI, p. 99. Professor Haupt very kindly allowed me to see his manuscript.

[3] Haupt cites as example of translation of names el Leǧǧūn (legio) for Megiddo, "place of troops." Nineveh had the by-name Mespila (Xenophon, Anab., 3, 4, 7), which Haupt equates with mushpîlu, "place of limestone."

The migration of Terah from Ur of the Chaldees to Harran must then be a reminiscence of a great movement of the Suti from Chaldaea up the Euphrates. This movement can only have begun after the Amorite migration was consummated. It was due no doubt to the constant pressure of additional Aramaean hordes coming from the Neǧd against Ur and Erech. In the ninth century we learn of a great many Aramaean tribes in Babylonia,[1] among whom are numbered especially the Puqudu (Pekod, Ezech. 23:23), Rapiqu, Damunu, Gambulu, and Tu'mânu (S A 1 ff.). Some of these groups may have infested Chaldaea at the time when the Suti were forced to emigrate, though the more immediate group seems to have been that of the Aḫlāme.

The westerly migration of these Aramaean tribes was facilitated by a great catastrophe which befell the Amorite realm. The first dynasty of Babylon was overthrown ca. 1760 by a terrible onset of the Hittites (G A § 454); for a chronicle informs us that in the days of Samsu-ditana the Hittites invaded the land of Akkad. It may be that the Hyksos invasion which befell Egypt is an organic part of the same general Hittite movement. The attack against Babylon was launched from the district of Ḫana on the Euphrates; for about 1600 B.C. Agum-kakrime records that he brought back the statues of Marduk and Ṣarpanit from the far land of Ḫana, whither they had apparently been carried in Samsu-ditana's time. This Hittite invasion must have destroyed the Amorite life in Ḫana as well as in Suḫu and Mari. Over Babylonia the Hittites seem to have gained no power of any duration, perhaps because of the Cassite invasion which simultaneously was pouring in from the north. And now the Aramaean movement, beginning with full vigor, swept on up the Euphrates, overcame the Hittites, overran Suḫu and Ḫana, and

[1] When they entered this region we do not know. G G 189 would find the Damunu and Puqudu present already in the days of Hammurapi because of the canal name Palag-Damanum and the city Pikudânu near Sirgulla.

followed the Ḫābūr and Balīḫ rivers up to the Tūr ʿAbdīn and the Euphrates as far as Carchemish and Syria.[1]

From the fourteenth century on the Suti are outstripped in importance by the Aḫlāme. The name, as has been suggested, is an Arabic broken plural from *ḫilmun* and means "allies." [2] The same root appears also in the name of the Ḫilimmu, a later Aramaean tribe (M V A G XI 226). They are first mentioned in the Amarna texts in a letter from Babylonia, so that it seems that they play the role in this region erstwhile played by the Suti. The supposed earlier mention of the Aḫlāme in Rim-Sin's day can scarcely be upheld (Klio VI 193). Shortly after 1400, in a letter of the Hittite king Ḫattusil to a king of Babylon, the "hostile Aḫlāmu" are referred to as having forced a suspension of the diplomatic correspondence (M D O G 35:22). In the next place Adadnirâri tells us that his father Arik-den-ilu (ca. 1350 B.C.) conquered the territory of the widespreading Guti, the region of the Aḫlāme and Suti

[1] Gen. 11; 10–26 reflects the progress of the Aramaean migration. If we deduct the three assuredly personal names Shelah, Reʿu and Terah, we have left a number of geographical termini. Arpakshad may be composed of *arba* and *kishadu* and may mean "four-shore country" (Z A 15: 255; D P 255), or *arpa* + *kishadu*, "borders of Chaldea" (G G 184). In either case it must apply to Babylonia. Eber means the shore land of the Euphrates north of Chaldea. (Cf. Ch. IV) Peleg is doubtless identical with Phalga at the mouth of the Ḫābūr (Proksch 80). Serug and Nahor appear in the towns of Sarugi (to-day Serûǧ) and Til-Naḫiri west of Harran (K A T 477 and cf. Ch. III). — Of much later origin is Gen. 10: 23. Hul (Havilah?) and Gether, "salt-plains" (G G 180), must represent east-Arabian districts. Uz refers to Damascus and the Syrian desert. (Has it any connection with the city of Az whence Gudea brought stone for mace-heads and which must have been in the Antilebanon?) Mash is Mons Masius or the Tūr ʿAbdīn region. It is identical with the mountain of Mash in the Gilgamesh epic, the Masīs or Musâs of the Alexander Romance, which name still clings to the Aghri Dagh (cf. Gressman Gilgamesh-Epos, p. 161).

[2] An important question that arises here is this: Did these Beduin call themselves Aḫlāme, or was it a name given to them by the Amoritish settlers on the Euphrates with whom they first came in contact? If the interpretation just given be correct, then the latter possibility is the more likely. The individual groups probably had their own tribal names. — True, the word Aḫlāme could be philologically equally well derived from the root *ʿalima* with Hommel G G 129.

(M K A no. 9 l. 15 f.). Since the Assyrians at this time scarcely can have fought the Aḫlāme in Babylonia, we must assume that they have now advanced far up the Euphrates into Mesopotamia. Indeed there are indications that the Aḫlāme were already penetrating northernmost Syria (OLZ '10:296). Adadnirâri himself tells us that he conquered the Kashiar region (Tūr 'Abdīn) and the stronghold of Harran as far as Carchemish. While he does not explicitly refer to the Aḫlāme, we must suppose that the campaign was really directed against them (M K A no. 11); for soon after we learn from Shalmaneser I (ca. 1300 B.C.) that the Aḫlāme are fighting as allies of King Shattuara of Ḫanigalbat on the upper reaches of the Euphrates near Malatia.[1] Valuable is the information which he gives that "from Taidi to Irridi the whole Kashiar region to the city of Eluḫat the stronghold of Sudi, the stronghold of Harran as far as Carchemish he captured their cities." (M K A no. 14 l. 18 f.) The Aḫlāme, apparently tributaries of Shattuara, thus held the Tūr 'Abdīn and the whole Balīḫ region including Harran and the district between Carchemish and Harran. Doubtless they also maintained themselves along the middle Euphrates.

A century and a half elapses until we again hear of the Aḫlāme. Ashur-resh-ishi (ca. 1140) relates that he destroyed their widespreading hosts, but unfortunately does not tell us where (A K A 19). His son Tiglathpileser I, however, is more explicit (Cyl. V 44 f.). He tells us that he marched "Into the midst of the Aḫlāme 'folk of Aram-land,' that were hostile to my lord Ashur." He describes their habitat further when he says that he devastated their country from the mouth of the Ḫābūr to Carchemish and drove the remnants of this people across the Euphrates. He himself ferried over the river on Keleks in pursuit of the defeated foe. At the

[1] Shalmaneser was hard pressed in this battle. He was cut off from water supply and caught in a narrow enfilade. The desperation of his troops, however, won the day. He himself fought with Shattuara at the point of the spear until sunset. He claims the capture of 14,000 men and many cities. He asserts that he slaughtered the Hittites and their allies the Aḫlāme like sheep.

foot of the Bishri mountains, i.e., Tell Bashar (P S B A'11:175), he captured six cities. On the left bank of the Sağūr he placed an Assyrian garrison in Pituru, which is probably identical with Tell Ghanīm below Ğerabis, and a second on the left bank of the Euphrates in Mutkinu, which must then be the modern Tell Ḥalâo (*l.c.*, p. 177). These were intended as frontier posts against the Aḫlāme. He evidently calls the Aḫlāme opposite the mouth of the Balīḫ Aramaeans because he recognizes their relationship to the people of the Kashiar and knows that they belong to one and the same racial group, for this Kashiar region is called in the "Broken Obelisk"[1] (AKA 128 ff.) mât Arimi, "land of Aramaeans," where the cities of Shaṣiri, Pauza,[2] Nabula, Shinamu and Ḫulza are mentioned. But Shupria, with the city of Murarir, east of Diarbekr, is also called an Aramaean land. Similarly Magrisi in the mountain of Iari at the great forks of the Ḫābūr, as well as Dūr-katlime on the lower Ḫābūr (cf. Chapt. VII) are described as being in the land of the Aramaeans.[3] On the other hand, the monolith of Ashurnazirpal from Kurkh (Rev. 47 A K A 240) calls the Aramaeans of Bīt-Zamani, in the Kashiar, Aḫlāme. We see therefore that by 1100 B.C. the cities along the Ḫābūr and Balīḫ, the right bank of the Euphrates from Suḫu to Carchemish, and the region of the Tūr 'Abdīn are explicitly described as settled by Aramaeans. The country west of Harran must also have received an influx of Aramaean population at this time. Oddly enough, the Assyrian records preserve absolute silence about this region.

We may safely say, then, that during the thirteenth century all of Mesopotamia was overrun by Aramaeans, and with the exception of a few Hittite-Mitanni enclaves, like Carchemish, it assumed Aramaean character. About this time the expression Aram

[1] In this inscription a successor of Tiglathpileser tells of the deeds of his great ancestor, as King and Budge have shown.

[2] The Uphaz of Dan 10: 5 ?

[3] At the time of Tiglathpileser IV the lower Tigris region near the gulf is called Land of Arumu. Cf. S A 115 f. (Surappu-Uknû). These people can only have come from the Neğd. The name "Aramaeans" is given to them by the Assyrian in recognition of their affinity to the more westerly people of the Kashiar and Syria.

Naharaim may have originated (Gen. 24:10). It is a modification of the Egyptian Naharin, and the Naḫrima of the Amarna days. In the Egyptian usage the term seems to include a considerable portion of Syria about as far south as Hamath. Müller held the name to be an abbreviation for "land of rivers," referring to the numerous streams that water it, Euphrates, Tigris, Balīḫ, Ḫābūr. (M A E 249 f.) When the Aramaeans came into possession of this region it could well be called the "river-Aram" in contrast to the other Aramaean seats. Meyer (G A I, 2 §§ 334, 463) interprets Naharaim as a locative of the singular "Aram on the Euphrates" and refers it to the region of the Osroene with Harran. The form Naḫrima, or Nârima in the Amarna letters supports this second view. Similar to this is the interpretation of Haupt (Z D M G 63:527) who translates "Euphrates-Aramaeans," holding that "Aram" only means the people and never a region. The expression Aram Naharaim probably disappeared after the ninth century when the Assyrians virtually wiped out the Aramaeans of this region. It belongs to the formative time of Aramaean principalities, as the analogy of Aram Zobah, Aram Beth Rehob reveals.

The origin of the name Aramaeans is shrouded in obscurity.[1] The earliest occurrences of it show that it is not the name of a region but of a people. The people is called Arimi, Aramu, Arumu; the second form is the most frequent and doubtless the original one, since the others represent merely vowel harmonization to the ending (Z A 27:283). Whether the mountain of Aruma mentioned by Tiglathpileser I (col. III 77), or the mountain city of Arma, of which Shalmaneser I (M K A no. 14 col. II 6 f.) says that he gathered its dust and poured it out in the gate of his city of Ashur as witness for the days to come, or the citadel of Arman at the headwaters of the Diyâla, or the god Armannu of the Rapiqu

[1] The theory of Haupt that Aramu comes from anʿāmun, "creatures" (Z D M G 61:194), I regard as unlikely. Not so impossible is the idea of Streck, Klio VI, that the name may go back to a divine appellation. Aram might then be regarded as an anagram of Amar. Cf. the fact that the Suti worshiped the god Amurru.

tribe near Bagdad (G G 190) have aught to do with this name cannot be decided with the means at our disposal.

The word "Aramu" has been interpreted as meaning "highlanders" from the Neǧd.[1] But we have seen that this people did not bear this name until they had settled in the Tūr ʻAbdīn regīon. Consequently we must prefer to call them "highlanders" of the upper Tigris and Euphrates. Since they had constant contact in that region with the Hittites, and since the latter at the time held dominion over Syria, it is possible that the name "Aramaeans" was transmitted southward through their agency. Hence we find those groups of the Aḫlāme which penetrated Syria after the Hittite debacle called by this appellation. Perhaps also the alternative translation of Aramu as "the exalted ones" was foremost in the consciousness of the Aḫlāme when they gave up their more ancient name in favor of the new.

[1] Grimme, Mohammed, '04: 15.

CHAPTER III

THE ARAMAEANS OF HARRAN

If Ur of the Chaldees is viewed by the Old Testament as the first station in the great advance of the Aramaeans, then Harran must be assigned the second place in importance. And indeed this harmonizes excellently with the clues that the inscriptions furnish; for, as we have seen, the advancing Aramaeans swerved from the Euphrates and followed its tributaries, the Ḫābūr and the Balīḫ. This was due no doubt to the presence of the Mitanni state west of the Balīḫ, which formed for a time a bulwark against further Aramaean invasion of this region. And, since the city of Harran was one of the most important cities of Mesopotamia, situated on a great trade route, it is but natural that it should be regarded from now on as a great Aramaean center from which the further northward and westward advance of this race radiated.

To the Harran district the Old Testament expression Paddan Aram clings. (Gen. 28:2, etc.) The term is by no means identical with Aram Naharaim, which is a larger geographical concept. The inscriptions furnish us with a land of Padan or Padin. Thus the Cassite king Agum-kakrime (ca. 1650) styles himself "king of Padan and Alman (=Arman?), king of the land of Guti." In this Padan[1] and Arman, Hommel sought to discover our Paddan Aram; according to him the name was carried by a Tigris migration of Aramaeans originally from Gir-su (which he interprets "road of the nomads" and of which he supposes Paddan Aram to be a translation) to the upper course of the Diyâla and then eventually to Harran (G G 190). But it seems unlikely that the Tigris migration was able to pass the Assyrian state in this angle; on

[1] A *rab ali* or "city chief" of Padânu is referred to in Rm 54, and in K 7376 Padânu is associated with the Ituai Aramaeans, A D D III 421.

the contrary, the mountain of Arman must be about the northernmost point reached by the Aramaean tribes of the Bagdad region. The Aramaeans of Harran must rather have crossed the Euphrates from the south, as we have supposed. The more commonly accepted view correlates Paddan Aram with the "field of Aram" (Hosea, 12:13), for in Aramaic and Arabic Paddan or Feddân means a yoke of oxen and then metaphorically the area that a yoke of oxen can plow in a day (D P 135). But Hosea's "field of Aram" has a much wider meaning than this and, furthermore, in Hosea's day Paddan Aram can no longer have existed owing to the expulsion of the Aramaeans from Mesopotamia by the Assyrians. More plausible is the view of Zimmern (cf. Gesenius-Buhl Buhl[15]) that Paddan is an older equivalent or a by-name of Harran, for padânu in Assyrian means "road" and is a synonym of harrânu. It seems to me, however, that Paddan Aram refers to a distinct city of Paddan, which is Aramaean in contrast to the eastern Padan. It is an example of how the priestly writing occasionally preserves very ancient material; for, while the other documents speak of Harran only, in the sense of the district belonging to the great capital of the Balīḫ, this tradition preserves the exact name of the town. And just S.W. of Harran there is a Tell Feddān in which, as Lagarde divined, our Paddan is preserved. Possibly a divergent tradition is contained in Gen. 24:10, "city of Nahor," which must be identical with the ancient Til-Naḫiri, lying probably a little to the west of Tell Feddān.

Tiglathpileser I does not seem to have had the Harran region under very firm control. True, he boasts (VI 61 f.) that he not only killed four monstrous wild bulls in the desert in the country of Mitâni near the city of Araziqi (the classical Eragiza on the left bank of the Euphrates, slightly south of the latitude of Aleppo, Sachau 133 f.), which is over against the land of Hatti, but also that he killed ten mighty elephants in the country of Harran and in the district of the Ḫābūr. But the "Broken Obelisk" relates (col. III 19) that he once made a raid from the land of Maḫirâni to the city of Shuppa, which is in the land of Harran.

Concerning the Harran Aramaeans we have received much enlightenment through an Assyrian census dealing with this district. It lists in detail the facts about each farm in a given district. It names the pater familias, and usually his sons, while the women are merely enumerated. The occupations of the various members of the household are tabulated and the condition of the holding in regard to area, cultivation and live-stock stated. The vineyards are described by the number of vines, roundly estimated, the herds according to hoof. Buildings, cisterns and ponds are likewise entered, and the name of the holding with its situation appended (H C 6f.). Since the inhabitants to a large percentage bear Aramaic names, this picture of their life must interest us. True, the census is from the seventh century and so objection might be raised to our making use of it in describing a period hundreds of years older. But the fact that the Aramaeans were never disturbed in Harran after the time of Tiglathpileser I as in regions further west, for the simple reason that they never rebelled against Assyria, leads us to believe that the conditions of later days correspond fairly to those of the patriarchal period.

In the principality of Harran are mentioned a number of smaller governmental units, called "qani" (H C 10). These are crystallized about places of importance and comprise a number of towns or suburbs. Thus the cities Harran, Dūr-Nabû, Tinunî, Tilabnî, and Ḫaurina stand at the head of such "qani." That of Harran included the towns Atnu, Badâni, Ianata, Saidi and Ḫânsûri, and the villages (*al she*) Arrizu and Kapparu. Several other cities were important enough to have dependent towns but were not seats of a qani. Thus Baliḫi has the towns Aanatâ, Bir-nâri and Ḫarnuṣaen belonging to it. Similarly Ḫasame has Gaduatâ, Sarugi has Ḫananâ and the village Laḫêili, Pidua has the village Akaru. Other cities mentioned in the census are Gadisê, Dimmeti, Ḫadatti, Ḫaluli, Ḫalṣu, Ḫamedê, Ḫumu, Immirîna, Nampigi, Diḫnunna, Rimusi, Tasume, Tillîni, Til-Naḫiri.[1]

[1] The identification of some of these places is difficult as we have no clues. Of some we shall hear again elsewhere. Dûr-Nabu maybe the Dûr north of

The personal names of the Aramaeans of Harran naturally are of absorbing interest;[1] for Oriental nomenclature is a mirror of the religious conceptions of the people, often, it is true, of a stage long outgrown, as in so many Old Testament names. For our purposes here this is especially valuable. In the names of the Harran district we find divinities not met with elsewhere, or if so, then under a slightly different guise. Very many names are compounded with a god Si', whom we meet also in the Palmyrene inscriptions and who is doubtless identical with Sin (H C 13). Thus we have Si'-dilîni, "S. hath set me free"; Si'-idri, "S. is my help"; Si'-aqabi, "S. is my reward"; Si'-manani, "S. hath counted me"; Si'-zabadi, "S. hath endowed." A further common divinity is Nashḫu, the Nusku of the Assyrians (H C 12); we find him in Nashḫu-dimri, "N. is my protection"; Nashḫu-gabri, "N. is my hero"; Nashḫu-sagab, "N. is exalted"; Nashḫu-sama'ani, "N. hath heard me"; Nashḫu-qatari, "N. is my rock." The only other instance of the form Nashḫu is found on a contract (C I S II t. 1, 35), where we have Nashḫu-aili, "N. is my strength," a sukallu or "overseer" of Niribi[2] about 645 B.C. (H C 12, 33). The god Adad is found in names like Adad-ḫutni, "A. is my protection." The god Ai (Aa, Ia), the great lunar deity of the Arabians (G G 95), is found in Ia-abbâ, "Ai is the father"; Iamaniai, "Ai is my right hand," Aa-ḫāli, "Ai is my uncle"; Ziri-ia, "My seed is Ai." Very peculiar is the occurrence of Al or Alla instead of the Assyrian ilu, "God"; thus we find Alla-sharru (malik?), "God is King"; Al Nashḫu-milki, "The god N. is my counsel." A further divinity is Ḫân, doubtless identical with the ancient deity of the Hittites, who has survived here from Mitanni days: Ḫân-dada, "H. is the

Harran at the site of the present Anaz (cf. Pognon, Inscriptions sémitiques, '08: 242 f.). Ḫamedê is doubtless Amid; Nampigi = Nappigu (Hierapolis); Ḫaurīna may be the Horrin south of Mardin (Sachau 400) or else Haura between Raqqa and Bālis (H C 49, 10).

[1] On the west-Semitic personal names cf. Hilprecht, Babylonian Expedition Series, A, vol. IX, p. 20 f., and especially A H T 75 f.

[2] The Nêrab near Aleppo, whence two old Aramaic inscriptions have come to us.

beloved"; Bîr-ḫânu, "Offspring of Ḫân." Unique are the gods Shêr and Têr. Thus we have the names Shêr-īlai, "Shêr is the god Ai" (G G 95), and Têr-nadin-apli (of which the last two elements are Assyrian), "Têr hath given a son." Têr is perhaps an Arabian deity and appears in the name of Abiate's father Têri in the Annals of Ashurbanipal (col. VIII 31), while Shêr may be identical with Sherua, the consort of Ashur (H C 18, 82). The goddess Até, a Hittite deity, is found in Atâ-idri, "Ate is my help." The Arabian and Aramaean Atar (=Ishtar) appears in Atar-idri, "A. is my help"; Atar-biʿ-di, "A. is my (curse-)remover." These two divinities were later merged into one, Atargatis, whose cult had its famous seat at Hierapolis (our Nampigi, Nappigu).

The life revealed by the Harran Census is chiefly agricultural (H C 19). Each cornland holding is described by "homers" of land, as is the case also in the Ḫana Tablets. The average holding had an area of 20–24 homers. Usually less than half of the area is mentioned as *arshu*, "cultivated"; the remaining doubtless was lying fallow. Each holding has one or more houses and an *adru* or "enclosure" (barn?). Sometimes a vineyard is attached to the holding, but occassionally it appears independently. The number of vines in the vineyards ranges from 2000 to 29,000. The account of the live stock shows that the pastoral stage no longer existed. Sheep herds count from 30 to 188 head, and only one goat herd of 58 head is mentioned. Of cattle the ratio is about one head to every ten homers of cultivated land. Isolated mention of the ass, the camel and the horse also occurs. The farms were hereditary holdings, and generally the previous owner is named along with the present. Women, too, could be holders, as a number of instances prove. The families are often remarkably small; the average of persons in one family is five. The monogamous system seems to have been the most common; in fifteen homes there are two wives and in six there are three. And here childlessness of the first wife may have been the cause for the departure from the rule. Thus, for instance, in four families with two wives there is no offspring at all.

No doubt the lateness of the period from which our census dates must be strictly borne in mind in drawing conclusions about earlier days. The conditions of agricultural life reflected here were not those existing among the nomadic Aḫlāme; an adaptation to Assyrian customs and laws has taken place. True, the transition from beduin to fellah is often rapid, and the Aramaeans round Harran doubtless accepted the ordered conditions immediately. But antiquity can only be claimed for the names whose Arabian character is plain.

Concerning the social conditions of the early Aramaeans of Harran we have a more ancient witness in Genesis 31, a chapter the value of which a little study will reveal. It is recorded there how the clan of Jacob,[1] abandoning the tribe of Laban, crossed the Euphrates and journeyed to Gilead. Jacob, in spite of his oppression by Laban, has grown rich and now seeks to secure his own camping grounds. But Laban with his "brothers" (vs. 23), i.e., clansmen, pursues Jacob and overtakes him at Gilead. The whole desert region from Gilead to the Euphrates is conceived of as Laban's territory. Jacob is accused by Laban of having stolen his divine images or teraphim. Jacob invites his accuser in the presence of "our clansmen" (vs. 32) to search the camp.[2] When the search is ended Jacob says, "What hast thou found of all thy property? Set it before my clansmen and thine to decide between us both."

The following un-Hebraic features should be noticed.

In the first place the women claim the right of inheritance of their father's property (vss. 14–15); in the Mosaic code this was

[1] It is commonly supposed that the name Jacob is an abbreviation for Jacob-el (cf. G V J I 418). Hommel finds a fitting analogy in the name of a Chaldaean Sheikh *Ya'qub-ilu*, which he interprets "God rewards" (G G 167). It may also be possible, however, to find the god Ya (Ai) in the first syllable of this name. We have just quoted the Harranian *Si'-aqabi*. The form *Ya-aqabi* would be equally possible. "Ya is the reward" or "Ya has rewarded" might then be the real meaning of "Jacob."

[2] As Procksch 351 shows, the incident in Gen. 31:34 f. is intended to cast ridicule on Aramaean idolatry. What kind of a god is that who allows an unclean woman to sit on him!

provided for only in extraordinary cases. Secondly, they claim that the wealth which Jacob has won is theirs and their children's, not *his* (vs. 16, they rebuff his claim in vs. 9). Un-Hebraic also is the character of vs. 33 f., where each woman has her own tent and is thus relatively independent. Among the Palestinian Hebrews Sarah is in the tent of Abraham; the harem is separated by a curtain from the men's room. But an older stage in the history of marriage is reflected here (Procksch 200), the Ṣadīka marriage,[1] where it lies within the woman's will to receive her husband's visit or not. Under this form of wedlock the man enters into the clan of the wife instead of the wife entering into the clan of the husband. That this conception really underlies our narrative is evidenced in vs. 43, where Laban, unable to answer the terrific arraignment of Jacob, boasts cruelly, "Mine are the daughters, mine the sons, mine the flocks, and all which thou seest is mine." He can do what he pleases with Jacob's family and possessions because he is the head of the family and his will is law; only out of goodness of heart does he yield to Jacob! But where in Israel has the father-in-law such authority? His control over his daughters ceases the moment the "*mohar*" or price is paid.

We must hold, then, that the early Aramaeans of Mesopotamia brought with them their primitive Arabian marriage customs, but dropped them as soon as they settled in established communities where the patriarchal forms prescribed by Hammurapi's laws were the rule. Indeed, as has often been pointed out, the relation of Abraham to his wives follows the precepts of Hammurapi. Abraham's family at Harran had therefore already adapted itself to these conditions. But Laban, who is more typical of the wandering Aḫlāme of the Syrian desert, still represents the truer Aramaic institutions brought along from Arabia.

Of old Aramaean or Arabian religion this chapter reveals but little, unless we regard the teraphim, which was probably a mask

[1] Cf. Robertson Smith, Kinship and Marriage in Early Arabia, p. 78.

for the face of the divine image and was worshiped as the giver of family welfare,[1] as strictly Aramaean. Oddly enough, it is mentioned only among the Hebrews and is never ascribed to the Canaanites; it is found, however, among the later Babylonians, who may have adopted it from the Aramaeans. (Ez. 21:26)

[1] Gressmann, Ursprung der Israelitisch-jüdischen Eschatologie, '05: 345.

CHAPTER IV

THE INVASION OF PALESTINE

THE Old Testament narrates how divine providence calls Abram away from Harran into a land set apart for him and his seed forever. Historically this reflects the movement of a great stream of humanity, upon which the migration of Abram is but a single wave.

Abram is called a Hebrew (Gen. 14:13). The origin and meaning of this latter name has been much discussed. The traditional view that 'Eber is the "region beyond" the Euphrates, and Hebrew therefore "the one from beyond," is unsatisfactory. Attention has often been called to the Assyrian expression Ebir-nâri, "region beyond the river," which became the official designation for the provinces west of the Euphrates from the time of Ashurbanipal on (S A 80). The Hebrew parallel, "Eberhannahar" (1 Kings 14:15), is not used in this fixed sense but merely means "land beyond the river," or perhaps still more simply "river country." This latter view is vindicated by the fact that Sargon (cf. Winckler 44 f.) translates the Edomite Ibr Naharân, which is in form identical with Eberhannahar, by Kibri-nâri, i.e., shoreland of the river (M V A G '98, 1, 55).[1] Furthermore 'Eber appears alongside of Ashur in Num. 24:24 as a similar concept, and if we interpret it as "shore-region" (of the Euphrates) we get an excellent sense. A similar meaning is directly offered by Isaiah 7:20, where the "shores of the river" Euphrates are referred

[1] G G 255 regards Ebirtān "beyond" as a synonym of kibir-nâri since the first part of the ideogram for the former word is Ki.A which ordinarily means kibru. He also calls attention to a city of Ibri in the vicinity of Babylonia.

to as "'Ebrei hannāhār." If we follow these clues we gain for "Hebrew" the sense "one from the shore of the Euphrates."[1] We must assume therefore that Abram migrated from Harran to Palestine before the name "Aramaean" became applied to the group to which he belonged. It is different with Jacob, who therefore belongs to a later stage.

It seems peculiar that the Abrahamic migration should seek southern Palestine instead of the more alluring region of Damascus or Hamath. The reason must be sought in the strength of the Amorite states in Coelesyria as well as in the Hittite advance. On the other hand, the weakness of Egyptian power in Palestine must have been such as to make an advance into that region especially alluring. The most suitable time for Abram's immigration was toward the end of the seventeenth century when the Egyptian power in Syria stood at zero owing to the internal troubles on account of the Hyksos (G V J I 90). Such a region as the Negeb, where Abram chiefly dwelt, was probably thinly populated and furnished an opportunity for strangers to settle.

The next migration of importance is that of Jacob-Israel. Jacob's earliest seat was in Gilead, at Mizpeh. The pressure of other Aramaean tribes from the north caused him great difficulty. In the thirty-first chapter of Genesis, a document of great historical value, as we have had occasion to point out, we are told of a treaty between Jacob and Laban.[2] In the later Leucosyrians we may have a remnant of the Laban tribe, for this name appears to be merely a translation of "Laban Aramaean" (Gen. 31:20; O L Z '07:547). The coloring of the story is accurate, for we learn that a dolmen or cairn is erected, which Laban calls Yegar Sahdūtha and Jacob, Ga'lēd. Dolmens, the megalithic monuments of the Indo-Europeans, are frequent in this region. What is more likely than that such a distinctive landmark of mysterious antiq-

[1] Similarly Guthe, Geschichte Israels, '14: 14. Another interpretation having plausibility is that of Spiegelberg, O L Z '07: 618, according to whom Hebrews means "Wanderstämme" or nomadic tribes.

[2] On the two versions cf. Procksch, p. 177 ff., 345 ff. Variance in details is no bar to the historicity of the treaty.

uity should serve as a boundary? Nor is there the least ground for supposing that the Aramaic name given the cairn by Laban is a late invention. For we have an analogy in an Aramaean *Yaghra* ("Hill") near the lake of Antioch (S B A '92, 333). Another version relates that they erected a pillar (Maṣṣēbāh) and called it Mizpeh. The historian's purpose is no doubt to inform us that the town of Mizpeh in Gilead, which may have been near the famous dolmen, is the site where the treaty was concluded. The actual terms of the treaty show a distinct inferiority of Jacob. They provide that Jacob shall take no further wives besides Laban's daughters. As Procksch has seen, this refers to an agreement on intermarriage between the two tribes, but only on the condition that further legitimate marriages (with Amorite women perhaps) be excluded. Jacob, being inferior in strength, has to accept these terms. His tribe entered into the negotiations doubtless because it was dependent on the good will of its powerful neighbors and also to insure a healthy growth for itself. With the related Esau tribes a similar agreement may have been reached as to the boundary.

Jacob, however, did not stay in Gilead, but changed his pasturage and came to the region of Shechem west of the Jordan. We may surmise the reason if we recall the fact that about this time the Amorite states in central Syria were again attaining to power. Under the leadership of Kadesh on the Orontes, the Syrian kingdoms presented a solid front against invasion and thus showed signs of great strength. The strong cities of the plain of Esdraelon seem to have belonged to the kingdom of Kadesh at that period. Seventeen campaigns against Syria are recorded by Thutmose III (from 1479 B.C. on). There is good reason indeed to believe that Kadesh at this time controlled Damascus and the Hauran; for the existence in the Mosaic age of Amorite kingdoms east of the Jordan — those of Og of Bashan and Sihon of Heshbon — evidences the Amorite power of expansion in the centuries previous. At any rate, the removal of Jacob and the cessation of all connection of the Hebrews with Aram hereafter seem to show that a power arose at that time in the country of Gilead which was the cause of both of these peculiar facts.

Jacob is called a "roving Aramaean" (Deut. 26:5). Because the Aramaeans migrated so much in those times, the name became almost synonymous with "Roamer."[1] This reminiscence concerning the origin of Jacob is all the more important since the Hebrews after him entirely lost their Aramaean character and became virtually Canaanites in language, custom and culture. It is remarkable that the memory of the old blood relationship and even details concerning the earliest common homes have survived.

A century after Jacob's time we stand in the Amarna age and learn of the great inroads of the SA.GAZ in Syria and of the Ḫabiri in Palestine. This age and its problems cannot be dealt with here. The question which alone concerns us is whether the Ḫabiri have anything to do with the Aramaeans.

As is now proven by the Boghaz-Koï Archives, the Ḫabiri and SA.GAZ are identical (Böhl 87). The west-Semitic equivalent of SA.GAZ (= ḫabbatu) seems to have been Shasu, "robber" (G V J I 520). The Ḫabiri can hardly be identical with the Hebrews, since, as we have seen, the patriarchal migration took place earlier and the Mosaic later, though philologically the names might well be correlated (Kn. 46 ff.). It seems more plausible to me, however, to explain the undoubtedly Semitic name from a Canaanitic root, "*ḫābar*," "to join" (= Akkadian *abâru*), so that Ḫabiri would mean "allies." In Arabic this root possesses a different meaning and therefore we must regard the name as an expression used by the Canaanites to describe the invaders and not as the real name of the people. And, indeed, it was almost necessary to invent such a name for them, since the preponderant element of the Ḫabiri seem to have been non-Semitic. There were Aryans[2] among them, and the name of this race occurs in Kn.

[1] Does Sennacherib Prism V 10 play upon this usage when he speaks of the "aramu ḫalqu u munnabtu"?

[2] The gods Mithra and Varuna are found in the Boghaz-Koï texts (M V A G '13, 4, 76 f.). Following a hint of Prof. J. A. Montgomery, I would see the deity Varuna in the Jebusite Arauna, 2 Sam. 24: 16 ff.

56:44 (where Ḫar-ri must be read instead of mur-ri [Böhl 17]). The names Shuwardata, Namyawaza, Biridashya (= Sanscrit Brhadashwa, "the one who owns a big horse") and many others in the Amarna letters are Indo-Germanic (G A § 468). On the other hand, there were also Hittites among the Ḫabiri in large numbers. Thus the chieftain Lapaya is of this stock, and in Abd-ḫipa of Jerusalem we have the divinity Ḫipa of the Hittites (Böhl 83). But there were also Aramaean elements included in the Ḫabiri,[1] especially the Suti of the eastern deserts. The Aḫlāme must also have been hammering at the gates of Syria, and their name, which is distinctly Arabian, forms a curious counterpart to Ḫabiri, since both mean "allies." It would be perfectly feasible if they were included among the "Ḫabiri."

Shortly after this time the Amorite state in central Syria was again revived. It had an important stronghold in Kadesh — not the great city on the Orontes, but that in Galilee (B A R III 71) — and it wavered between allegiance to the Hittites, who are now established in the northern Kadesh, and the Egyptians, seeking protection with one against the other (G V J I 521). Through it the Amorite states east of the Jordan must have been reinvigorated. Seti I of Egypt (1292 B.C.) storms Kadesh, and thus subjects the Amurrû state. Operations against the Amorites east of the Jordan appear certain from the erection of a stele of victory in the Hauran at Tell esh-Shihāb.

From now on a great struggle ensues between the Egyptians and the Hittites. It was finally concluded by the famous treaty between Ramses II and Ḫattusil, a cuneiform copy of which has recently been found by Winckler at Boghaz-Koï, the capital of the Hittite empire (M V A G 13, 4, 101 f.). The Amorite state now enjoyed a quasi-independence under Hittite suzerainty; its king Bente-shina became the brother-in-law of Ḫattusil. Indeed, it seems to have extended its influence quite far into the Syrian desert; for we learn that Bente-shina made a raid upon Babylonian territory, since he could not collect the thirty talents of silver

[1] Similarly Clay, Cassite Names, p. 42 f.

which the city of Agade owed him, and it is doubtful whether his victims' complaint to Ḫattusil was of avail.

The terrible catastrophe which put an end to the Hittite empire as well as to the Amorite state occurred in the time of Merneptah whose accession took place in 1225 B.C. The onset of the maritime peoples was so terrific that even the Egyptians were barely able to ward them off. Among them are the Philistines. Ramses III finally, in a great battle by land and by sea, hurled them back and unified Palestine once more under Egyptian rule (B A R IV § 59ff.). In the country east of the Jordan, however, the Amorite principalities still existed.

At this time and on this background occurs the arrival of the Israel tribes in the promised land. They are only able to enter it after circumventing Edom [1] and Moab, and then striking at the Amorite kingdom of Heshbon under its king Sihon (G V J 545f.). This state, together with that of Og in Bashan, are the main remnants of former Amorite power. In Numbers 32:39 Makir is driving Amorites out of Gilead.

That the relations between Moab and Ammon, who are the purest of Aramaean stock so that they can boast of their origin from Lot's daughters (Procksch 129) and the Aramaeans of Mesopotamia, continued to be friendly, we may infer from the fact that Balak of Moab summons an Aramaean seer from Pethor on the Euphrates to "curse Israel." Mesopotamia is there expressly described as the land of Balaks, "sons of his people," i.e., of the related Aramaeans (Num. 22:5). This opinion, even if it be only that of the Hebrew writer, is important because it shows that the Moabites were considered an Aramaean people. The Hebrews, however, through intermingling with Hittites, Canaanites, Cushites and others, have lost their Aramaean character, so that Moab does not regard them as closely related

[1] Z D M G 63:528 corrects king of Edom, Num. 20:14, into king of the Aramaeans. That the Edomites were merely an Aramaean tribe I regard as assured. *Ibid.* 506, the correction of Aram, Num. 23:7, into Edom is disputed. Haupt here regards Aram as the region S.E. of Elath, which in the Koran, 89:6, appears as the Iram of the Adites.

to itself. From the Assyrian inscriptions we have learned in a former chapter that Tiglathpileser I conquered Pitru (=Pethor) on the Euphrates, and placed Assyrian garrisons in Pitru and Mutkinu as outposts against the Aḫlāme. Tiglathpileser ruled about 1100 B.C. If the exodus of Israel took place under Merneptah about 1220 B.C. (G V J 537), and if a stay in the desert is assumed for forty years, we would have the date 1180 for the coming of Balaam from Pethor. How remarkably this harmonizes with the fact that the Aramaeans at this time actually held Pitru! This speaks highly in favor of our tradition.

The Aramaean home of Balaam [1] is substantiated by the ancient poem 23:7 f., "From Aram Balak caused me to be brought, from the mountains of Qedem the Moabite king." Since Sinuhe, the Egyptian, journeys from Gebal inland to Qedem, its location is east of Byblos. It probably refers to the region beyond Damascus (G V J 66). In Genesis 29:1 the term is applied to the country from Palmyra to the Euphrates (*ibid.* 369). In the vicinity of Qedem, or perhaps within it, lay the land of Ya'a, over which the Amorite king Ammienshi makes Sinuhe ruler; Kittel and Ranke locate this near the lake of Tiberias.[2] In these very regions, as we shall soon see, and about this very time new vistas of Aramaean life and history are unfolding.

[1] The Mesopotamian character of Balaam is proven by Daiches, Hilprecht Anniversary Volume, p. 60 ff., from the conformance of his soothsaying methods with the Babylonia ritual. Even the title of Balaam, Num. 24:16, "Hearer of the words of God, knower of the knowledge of the most high," reminds one of the Babylonian, "the wise man, the knower who keeps the mystery of the great gods" (Zimmern, Ritualtafeln, 118, 19).

[2] A land of Ya' in the region of Iadnana is mentioned in Sargon's Display inscription, l. 145. Iadnana is usually identified with Cyprus.

CHAPTER V

THE RISE OF THE ARAMAEANS IN CENTRAL SYRIA

The great onset of the Indo-Europeans which shattered the Amorite and Hittite power in Syria paved the way for the Aramaean possession. The Biqâ', especially, suffered from the vandalism of the invaders; for the Egyptians tell us that the land became as if it had never existed (B A R IV § 64). To a large extent the population must have been annihilated. The mighty strongholds which had stood many a siege and were built with consummate skill, like Kadesh and others, must have succumbed finally to starvation and disease. Perhaps only in the most sheltered mountain retreats did the inhabitants remain undisturbed.

Already at the beginning of the Indo-European movement, the Aramaean won important positions from which he could at the right moment stretch out his hand to the country's heart. For, as Müller has shown, his name is not unfamiliar to the Egyptian of the time of Merneptah. One of this Pharaoh's officials has made a record of the sending of messages "to the city of Merneptah which lies in the territory of *A-ira-mau.*" This can only be Aram. But in reality he means Amor. It is a scribal error, but it shows that the Aramaeans were already within the scope of Egypt's official cognizance (M A E 222).

The Aramaean invasion of Syria, then, synchronizes with the entrance of the children of Israel into Palestine. Viewed from the distance both are identical; it is one great wave, that, coming from the Arabian desert, floods the land, and inaugurates a new period of its history.

In Syria the Aramaeans were at first too busy in establishing themselves, to bother much about their neighbors.[1] This is reflected in Judges 18:7, 28, according to the LXX reading, where we learn that the dwellers of Laish lived peacefully apart, far from the Phoenicians to whom they belong and without relation to *Aram*. Thus, at the time when the Danites settled at Laish, Aram (perhaps the principality Beth Ma'acah may be meant) was already a fixed geographical terminus for the region north of Palestine.

At the time of Saul, ca. 1025, we find several Aramaean kingdoms definitely established on the edge of Canaan. For in 1 Samuel, 14:47 we read that Saul warred "against Moab, and against the Ammonites, and Aram Beth-Rehob[2] and the king of Zobah." The chronicler has no exact information and so does not tell us who the king of Zobah was; but that is no reason for impugning the accuracy of his statement.

The location of Beth-Rehob may be fixed with fair certainty as north of Ammon. The relation between the two states was always a close one. The Rehobite Ba'sa is later the leader of the Ammonites in the battle of Qarqar (W G I I 141). In the ruined city of Rīḥāb, discovered by Schumacher in 1900, forty kilometers east of Ağlūn and fifty north of 'Ammān — the old Rabbath Ammon — is to be sought, according to Guthe, the capital of Beth-Rehob.[3] It lay between the Argob and the upper reaches

[1] A vague reminiscence of a first warlike conflict between Aram and Israel seems to be preserved in Jud. 3: 7–11. A priori such an invasion as that of Cushanrishathaim is not to be dismissed as impossible. How suddenly such attacks may come, we observed in the case of the Hittite onset against Akkad in the days of Samsu-ditana. That Mesopotamia was at this time (ca. 1150) called Aram Naharaim we have held most plausible. Perhaps, following Marquard's example, we should separate the name of this king into Cushan ra's (or "chief") of 'Ataim. There may well have been a locality 'Ataim in old Mitanni, a place where the divinity Atê was worshiped. A still further possibility might be to hold 'Ain an error for Heth. Then Cushan would be a Hittite chieftain, perhaps from Carchemish. True, the name Cushan arouses suspicion (cf. Hab. 3: 7).

[2] Text emended: Edom into Aram. Beth-Rehob supplied from LXX. W G I. I. 143.

[3] Protestantische Realenzyklopädie, 3d ed. by Hauck, Vol. 21, p. 703.

of the Jabbok river, and doubtless extended east to the Zalmon range.[1] It is the most easterly of the early Aramaean principalities.

More problematic is the conflict of Saul with Zobah, if this state lay, as we hold, to the west of Damascus in the Biqâ'. But unless we proceed radically as Winckler does (W G I I 142), it is difficult from our tradition to locate it anywhere else. If Zobah really is to be sought in Sūf, thirty kilometers west of Rībāb (Guthe, *l. c.*), then it is indeed strange that in the Hebrew conquest of Palestine, and in the extensive geographical lists, this important city is not mentioned (S A 141). On the other hand if Zobah be the Biqâ', and thus the heir of ancient Amurrû, it is perfectly possible that its power and influence should have extended into the country east of the Jordan, so as to conflict with the ambitions of Saul. That is only analogous to the conditions centuries previous, when the Amorite state expanded into the trans-Jordanic territory. Indeed just as the principality of Sihon at Heshbon was founded and colonized from the Biqâ', so also must the Aramaean state of Beth-Rehob and its sisters have been daughters of Zobah.

As Halévy showed,[2] the word is derived from "*Zehobah*" — "copper, bronze," and must be an appellative with the meaning "the copper country." Thus copper must be a notable product of this region. Now this is peculiarly true of the Lebanon district, where there are large deposits of this mineral (E K XVII 1063). And in this connection it must be recalled that we have a city of Chalcis (i.e., "copper") as the capital of the later kingdom of Ituraea which was situated in the Marsyas plain. This Chalcis must be the ancient Zobah.[3] And indeed Eupolemus

[1] Others — to my mind erroneously — localize it in the region of Caesarea Panias, S A 76.

[2] Mélanges, 1874, p. 82. Halévy's combination of Zobah-Chalcis with the Nuḫashshe of the Aramna days fails. The latter is probably the northern Chalcis (Kinnesrîn) near Aleppo, Kn. 1104 f. (Cf. next note.)

[3] From the cuneiform inscriptions a province of Ṣubatu (Ṣubutu, Ṣupite) is known, which has long been identified with our Zobah. Winckler seeks it south of Damascus (W G I, I 141; K A T 61). But the arguments from

(ca. 150 B.C.), in recounting the wars of David, substitutes "Ituraeans" for Zobah, showing thereby that a very definite and fixed tradition placed Zobah in this locality (S A 145). In the magnificent ruins of il-'Anǧar in the Biqâ' we perhaps have the site of Chalcis and the old capital of Zobah.[1]

After the accession of David, however, the real struggle with the early Aramaean states of Syria is begun. It was provoked by the troubles with Ammon. The king of the latter state, Hanun ben Nahash, shamefully insulted and abused David's ambassadors. It is very possible that the Ammonites were directly encouraged in such insolence by the Aramaeans, who clearly foresaw the necessity and inevitability of a conflict with the rising Hebrew state and preferred to have the aid of Ammon in this eventuality. As soon as the latter perceived that David was not inclined to submit to such an insult, it summoned the aid of Zobah and Beth-Rehob as well as of Ma'acah, a small Aramaean state adjoining Beth-Rehob and located in the Ǧōlān directly east and north of the lake of Hūle. (2 Sam. 10.) In this conclave of Aramaic states one only is omitted — the small Geshur, southerly neighbor of Ma'acah, and on the eastern side of the lake of Galilee. The relations between Geshur and the Hebrews on the west side of the lake appear to have been peculiarly intimate.

Ashurbanipal's Annals, VII, 114, are not convincing. This king tells us that he defeated the Arabs in Edom, in the pass of Yabrūd, in Ammon, in Ḫaurīna, in Seir, in Ḫarge, in Ṣubitu. There is no geographical sequence maintained in this summary, however; for from Ḫaurīna (Ḥawārīn north of Damascus) he jumps back to Seir. Not much more help is given by the geographical Catalogue, II R 53. Here a Ṣubat (al) Ḫamattu appears in Rev. 41 between Hamath and Sam'al, a Ṣubatu between Hadrach and Sam'al in Rev. 60, and again between Hadrach and Ṣimirra in Rev. 73. I hold that this Ṣubatu has nothing to do with our Zobah-Chalcis in the Biqâ', but that it was confused with it by the chronicler (2 Chron. 8: 3 f.) when he speaks of Hamath-Zobah. This Ṣubat (al) Ḫamattu (or Ṣupite, Ṣubutu) I seek in the northern Chalcis (Qinnesrīn south of Aleppo). Here the Arabian campaign as well as A B L no. 414, in which a prefect of Ṣupite reports concerning conditions in the province and relations to the Arabs (A O F I 465), is readily comprehended.

[1] Cf. Kiepert, Handbuch der Alten Geographie, '78: 164. Droysen, Geschichte des Hellenismus, III, 290, however, seeks Chalcis in Zaḥleh.

(2 Sam. 3:3, 13:37.) It was this close affiliation with Geshur, no doubt, which prevented that state from siding with the Aramaean coalition.

The Aramaeans of Zobah and Beth-Rehob together furnish 20,000 men. That the troops of the southernmost and northernmost Aramaean kingdoms should be counted as a unit is indeed peculiar; it may find its explanation, however, in the fact that Hadadezer is called (2 Sam. 8: 3 "ben Rehob," which means "Rehobite"; cf. W G I I 141). He is thus a native of Beth-Rehob, and after becoming king of Zobah, is the special protector of the land of his birth, and not merely its suzerain. Ishtob,[1] king of Ma'acah, arrives with 12,000 men. Joab, as David's field marshal, sets out to attack the coalition. Like Rameses before Kadesh, he is lured into an ambuscade, and his retreat is cut off. The Israelites hurl themselves first against the Aramaeans and through the bravery of desperation their attack becomes irresistible; the Aramaeans are put to flight. And when Joab now turns against the Ammonites, these, seeing that they are deserted by their allies, retreat to Rabbah's sheltering walls. But just as the "victorious" Rameses at Kadesh was glad to return home without molesting the city, so also Joab is satisfied to go back to Jerusalem into winter quarters. The first pitched battle between Hebrew and Aramaean of which we have record has thus resulted in a draw.

But Hadadezer was not willing to accept the verdict of the battle before Rabbah. He had not displayed his full force. Now he summoned help from "the Aram which is beyond the river." It is not at all impossible that his authority extended so far, for we have the Amorite state of Benteshina's day whose rule extended far into the Syrian desert toward Babylon, as an analogy. And just at this time Assyria was entirely dormant. But it is sufficient

[1] Ishtob seems to be a personal name, K H K 248. Those who prefer the traditional "men of Tob" may find the site of Tob in eṭ Ṭayyibe near Edrei. The list is not intact; 2 Sam. 10: 16 proves that Hadadezer must have been mentioned and probably also the king of Beth-Rehob.

to assume that the common blood relationship made mutual aid against other peoples a matter of course, according to sound Oriental principle "I and my brother against the son of my uncle, and I and the son of my uncle against the stranger." Hadadezer's forces are placed under the command of his field marshal Shobak.[1] So momentous is the impending struggle for the Hebrews that David himself takes command of his host. He crosses the Jordan (10:17) and marches to Helam [2] which must have lain at the head waters of the Yarmuk river and is probably identical with the Alema of I Maccabees 5:26 (Z A W '02, 137); a reminiscence of it might possibly be seen in 'Ilma on the Wadi il-Ghār not far from the caravan road Damascus — Sheikh Miskīn over which the Aramaeans were likely to come. At Helam David's leadership gained the victory. The Aramaeans were crushingly defeated and their commander Shobak slain. Hadadezer's allies from Mesopotamia immediately concluded a peace with David, and so the latter was able to besiege and capture Rabbah undisturbed.

The effect of the battle upon Zobah's prestige was disastrous. The princes of Mesopotamia had lost all respect for him, and therefore it was necessary to reëstablish his position of authority. Consequently we learn (8:3) that he goes to retrieve his power at the "river." [1] David appreciates that Hadadezer is only postponing further hostilities toward Israel until a more opportune season, and therefore decides to strike Hadadezer once more (Z A W '07, 16 ff). If we are told that the battle took place near Hamath (1 Chr. 18:3) we must regard this as unlikely. The fortresses along the Orontes would have blocked the pursuit of Hadadezer. David could not have passed them so swiftly. Nor is it likely that Hadadezer's expedition led through the territory

[1] Shofak in 1 Chron. 19: 16. I suspect that Shobak is an error for Sâkap, or Sa'kap, an apparently Aramaic Mesopotamian name (cf. A D D III 284), in which case the form Shofak would be the better. It is also possible, however, that the name contains the god Aku, like Shadrach (Shudur-Aku = "command of Aku").

[2] Helam has been identified by others with Ḫalman (Aleppo), but this seems too far north.

of the Hittite kindgoms to the north. The Aramaeans subject to him must have been the Aḫlāme opposite the mouth of the Balīḫ. Therefore an expedition thither would most naturally follow the highway from Damascus to Palmyra and Raqqā. Since David through his victory over Ammon and its northern neighbors could move about unhindered in Bashan, it is reasonable to conclude that from this base he launched his raid and intercepted Hadadezer east of Damascus. Under this supposition the entire picture receives a more rational aspect. The battle may then have taken place near Atera just east of where the Palmyra road diverges from the road to Hamath. It resulted in a complete victory for David.[1] An auxiliary force that came up from Damascus was likewise dealt a crushing blow. David successfully followed up his victories by subjecting Damascus and occupying it for the present by instituting prefects in it, a measure that shows David's resentment of Damascus interference (Z A W '07, 18).

But David went still further — he invaded the Biqâ' from the east, and so penetrated into the heart of Hadadezer's realm. Two cities of Zobah are mentioned (8:8) — Berothai and *Tebah* (LXX 1 Chron. 18:8). M T erroneously reads Betah and the book of Chronicles for Berothai substitutes Kun. If we could identify these places we should know exactly the location of Zobah. Berothai is mentioned in Ezechiel's description of Israel's boundaries (47:16); the northern border is there defined as extending from the sea over Berothah and Sibraim, between Damascus and Hamath, to Hazar Enon on the edge of the Hauran. Berothai's location in the Lebanon is thus assured. And its site is doubtless preserved in Brêtan N. E. of Zahleh (Z D P V 8:34) while Kun

[1] The figures of the dead and captured in our present text are scarcely trustworthy. Reliable, however, is the statement about the horses, 8: 4. The meaning "hamstring" for 'iqqēr is unsatisfactory, however. Procksch 267 suggests "castrate." But the best sense here is "cut off," i.e., slaughter. David is obeying the precept in Deut. 17: 16, which prescribes that a king must not have many horses. Thus he only retains one hundred and slaughters the rest. After David's time no king would have thought of such a thing. This speaks for the antiquity of our tradition.

is to be found in the classical Conna, a few hours distance north on the Homs road. Tebah is found also among the bastard Aramaeans in Genesis 22:24. It is mentioned in Papyrus Anastasi after Kadesh (in Galilee M A E 173) and before Gebal and Bērūt and also occurs in the Armarna letter (Kn. 179) as Tubiḫi alongside of Amurrû; and its name is, as has been supposed, perhaps contained in et-Tuffaḥ a district east of Sidon. Thus a satisfactory location for Hadadezer's cities in the Lebanon district may be found. And our traditions expressly emphasize the fact that large stores of copper were captured (2 Sam. 8: 8). David thereupon returned home and performed the duty of every pious Oriental King, — he gave votive offerings to his god. As such are mentioned the golden shields of Hadadezer's grandees, and other valuable objects (8: 7, 11). Before this, however, — perhaps at Conna, — he received the embassy of the Hittite king Toi of Hamath (8:10). The latter's own son[1] came with presents for the King of Israel and congratulated him on his victory over Zobah. Since the poor Hittite had been the victim of Zobah, as well as of Aramaean inroads from the Euphrates region, we may assume that his congratulations were sincere. The political significance of his act, however, is the acknowledgment by Hamath of Israel's supremacy in Syria. True this hegemony was only short lived but to its brilliance later centuries looked back with awe and, wonder, and dreamed of its restoration as the future's ideal.

[1] He is called Joram in 1 Sam. and Hadoram in 1 Chron. According to Dussaud, R A '08: 224, the original name probably was Hadad-ram.

CHAPTER VI

THE EARLY KINGS OF DAMASCUS

DAMASCUS, "the eye of the world" as Julian the Apostate surnamed it, lies in a rich and beautiful oasis formed by the river Barada. This stream, descending from the rugged Antilebanon, and called by the Greeks "Chrysorrhoas" — river of gold — was famous in antiquity for its cold and clear waters. Thus Naaman, the Aramaean, at the thought of the muddy Jordan, scornfully cries, "Are not the Amana and the Pharpar, rivers of Damascus,[1] better than all the waters of Israel?" Indeed these rivers have made it possible for the city to have such a wealth of gardens and parks, which are already mentioned by the Assyrian annals, and which to the Arab are the image of paradise. But to the east of Damascus lies the sandy desert, traversed only by the caravan roads to the distant Euphrates, and to the west the snow-crowned Hermon and the Antilebanon hold watch over the "pearl of the east."

Damascus in the Amarna days [2] does not seem to have possessed

[1] Amana is really the Antilebanon range (called by the Assyrians Amanana), Cant. 4: 8, and by metonomy the river descending from this mountain, the Barada. The Pharpar is probably the Aʿwağ; the old name still survives in the Ğebel Barbar. Expository Times, '01, 2, 219 f.

[2] Damascus is called "Dimashqu" in the Amarna texts. Haupt, Z D M G 63: 528, assumes a form Dar-mashqī as original and translates "settlement in a well-watered region." It seems to me, however, that Dimashqu is the older form and is composed of di and mesheq. Cf. Di-zahab, "the one of gold," Deut. 1: 1. Cp. also the late form Dummesheq with Arabian names like Dhu-Raidān. Mesheq means "acquisition," "gain," and thus Dimashqu must be "the one of acquisition," "place of gain," a suitable name for a city situated on a commercial highway. The Assyrians write for Damascus the

much importance. It remains under the control of the Amorite state and then of Zobah until subjugated by David. The city appears to have come into Aramaean hands during the thirteenth century, for in the Rameses III list of cities it is written *Tiramaski* (M A E 234). This writing shows that the Aramaic "Darmeseq" was already coming into vogue. The new population proudly called the city "*dar*" or Fortress" rather than merely "place of Mesheq." The Hebrews, it is true, retained the old form "Dimashqu" only slightly aramaized as Dammeseq down to the time of Isaiah, if we may trust the Massoretic tradition.

For a brief period the Aramaeans of Damascus and Coelesyria seem to have recognized the suzerainty of the King of Israel. If we read in 1 Kings 4:21 that kingdoms as far north as the Euphrates brought Solomon presents and were subject to him or more definitely (4:24) that his power extended from Thipsach (Thapsacus on the Euphrates; to-day Tel il Thadayain A E T 142) to Gaza, this is perfectly comprehensible; for he who ruled Amurrû exercised power also over the regions east toward Babylonia as we have seen in the case of Benteshina's state. Because of the weakness of Assyria, and through this alliance with Egypt and Tyre Solomon was the greatest ruler in Syria during his day. And if our assumption that the defeat of Hadadezer took place on the Palmyra road be correct, then the mention of Thapsacus becomes still more credible and even the late statement (2 Chr. 8:4) that Solomon fortified Tadmor (Palmyra) is plausible. The latter was then a military base from which the roving Aramaeans were

ideogram SHA-IMERI-SHV. Pognon (Inscriptions Sémitiques, 177) suggests that IMERI stands for the god Amar, for this ideogram means both "ass" and "Amaru" (Brünnow, 4905). Since "ass" was then also written in other ways, SHA-NITA-SHU and other forms came to be mechanically used for Damascus. Cf. also Clay, Miscellaneous Inscriptions, p. 2, and "Amurru," p. 130. Haupt, however, Z D M G 69: 169, defends with skill the interpretation that the ideogram means "city of asses." KUR, which interchanges with ālu, "city," before the ideogram, he argues, means "mountain" and refers to the Antilebanon at the foot of which Damascus lay. Along the western slope of this range led a road which was mainly traveled by caravans using asses as beasts of burden.

kept in check. Solomon's commercial control [1] of all the important highways of Syria lent his authority an immense support.

But during Solomon's lifetime a retrogression of his power took place. An adversary arose for him in the person of Rezon (Hezion?) [2] who had fled from the presence of his lord Hadadezer, king of Zobah (1 Kings 11: 23–25) at the time of David's Aramaean wars. He gathered about himself a troop of adventurers, and perhaps with the aid of large Beduin contingents seized Damascus. The moment that a strong personality was able to establish an independent kingdom north of Palestine, Israel's control of Colesyria was of course at an end. Hamath, Thapsacus and Palmyra adapted themselves immediately to the new conditions. Rezon we are told became a thorn in Solomon's flesh, and was "king of Aram." If we may trust our narrative, Damascus from now on became "Aram" par excellence.

The division of the kingdom under Rehoboam gave Damascus abundant opportunity for consolidation of power. Israel and Judah were too busy with their own affairs to pay much attention to Syrian politics. Damascus doubtless forced the hard pressed Jeroboam to make important concessions. But we have little light on the events in Damascus at this time. In 1 Kings 15: 18 there appears to be preserved the succession of the kings in Damascus; the order given is Hezion — Tabrimmon — Benhadad.

[1] 1 Kgs. 10: 28 f. seems to claim that he imported chariots and horses from Egypt and transmitted them to the kings of the Hittites and Aramaeans. K A T 239 discredits this, although the frequent mention of Kusaean horses in the letters might be cited in its support. Böhl 25 offers a novel interpretation. He takes Mōṣā (vs. 28) as the starting point of the import and translates, "the export of horses *for* Solomon took place from Muṣri (Cappadocia) and Que (Cilicia)" and was accomplished through the agency of the kings of the Hittites and Aramaeans.

[2] LXX in 11: 23 has Esron. This would be the equivalent of Hezron. It has been supposed (cf. K H K *ad loc.*) that Hezion is an error for Hezron. But the converse seems more likely to me. I regard Hezion as the name of the first king of Damascus. The form Rezon is secondary. Hezion is vouchsafed as a good Aramaean form by the Mesopotamian Ḫaziānu, A D D no. 61 rev. 8. Winckler's view, A T V 62, that the original name was Hazael, I regard as unlikely.

Apparently Hezion is identical with Rezon. About Tabrimmon [1] we know nothing. With Benhadad the Hebrew king Baasha (914–890) seems to have formed an alliance in order to safeguard himself against attack from the north.

But alas for Israel! When the king of Judah Asa (917–876) was being badly worsted by Baasha he sent what was left of the temple treasure, plundered not long before by Sheshonq (1 Kings 14:25–26), to Benhadad, pleading with him to break his alliance with Israel. The wily Aramaean was easily persuaded. Swiftly he attacked Baasha from the north, capturing Iyon in the fertile Merǧ ʻAyūn west of Mt. Hermon, Dan, Abel beth-maacah, and all Cinneroth (the rich plain of il Ghuwēr on the west shore of the lake of Galilee) and all Naphtali, including such important cities as Kedesh, Hazor, Merom, and Zephath. The effect upon Baasha was immediate, for he ceased his operations of fortifying Ramah, north of Jerusalem. The summoning of Benhadad by Asa, while effective, was none the less extremely short sighted, as intelligent Judaeans realized and as the Seer Hanani openly declared (2 Chr. 16:7–10). It was a betrayal of his own race and bred an animosity which later resulted in an alliance of Israel and Damascus against Judah.

It was but natural that Aramaean statesmen hailed with glee any request for intervention in Palestine. If Israel desired the assistance of Aram it could obtain it only in return for concessions in respect to the trade route to Akko; and if Aram had cause to war against Israel its first object was to seize the territory along this route. The attack upon Baasha safeguarded this caravan road almost completely; for the region west of Rama, not occupied by Benhadad, belonged to the tribe of Asher, which had come

[1] The name means "Rimmon is wise" (A T V 74). Rimmon is the god of the Aramaeans of Damascus (cf. 2 Kings 5:18). Rimmon or Rummān means "pomegranate." The god with the pomegranate is designated by this symbol as the spouse and brother of Ishtar. He is identical with Hadad. The Akkadians, it appears, borrowed Rimmon from the west and called him Ramman, popularly connecting the name with ramâmu, "to thunder" (A A 97 f.).

largely under Canaanite influence (cf. Judges 5:17) and naturally welcomed all trade from the east. Thus Benhadad I looms up in history as a figure of importance, and a ruler of great vigor and skill.

Benhadad must have died during the early years of Omri's reign (899–877). For if we learn from 1 Kings 20:34 that the father of Benhadad II wrested from Omri a number of cities, and forced him to make commercial concessions, this can hardly refer to Benhadad I. It would be odd indeed to find in the Semitic world a son bearing the same name as his father. An unknown king — possibly the Rezon of 1 Kings 11:23 who was confused with Hezion — must have ruled in Damascus as the contemporary of Omri. He forced the Hebrew king to give Syrian merchants a quarter of their own at Samaria. Since the Aramaeans controlled the highway to Akko it was but natural that they should take advantage of their predominance to capture the Israelitic trade market. Through a clever stroke of diplomacy, however, Omri succeeded in offsetting this defeat; he renewed the covenant with Phœnicia (18:18 G V J 334). This naturally tended to keep Damascus in check. The alliance was cemented still further by the marriage of Omri's son and successor Ahab (877–853) to the daughter of Ethbaal, king of the Sidonians (877–876).

A further restraint upon the Aramaeans was the advance of Assyrian power, which began to loom up like a thundercloud. After centuries of lethargy Ashur had once more awakened and was treading the pathway to a great destiny. Under the mighty Ashurnazirpal it was striking at the Aramaean and Hittite states to the north. In some manner the first contact between Israel and Assyria must have taken place in Omri's day, for henceforth Israel appears in cuneiform records as Bīt-Ḫumri or "house of Omri" and its kings are often called mâr-Ḫumri, literally "son of Omri," but really meaning "son of Bīt-Ḫumri," i.e., Israelite. If Omri sought aid against Damascus he received none, for Ashurnazirpal evaded this city's sphere of influence.

Since Omri's later days Israel was nominally a vassal of Aram.

Perhaps Ahab now neglected to pay tribute and so provoked his suzerain. In the meantime Benhadad II had come to the throne in Damascus. With startling suddenness the Aramaean appears before the gates of Samaria accompanied by 32(?) vassal kings and their cohorts (1 Kings 20). The number is doubtless exaggerated and should perhaps be reduced to eleven; for Damascus only had twelve allies (including Israel) in 854. Even then it seems astonishing that so powerful a league should be brought into action against Israel. And indeed we would be at a loss to account for this fact if it were not for the light shed on Syrian affairs by the cuneiform inscriptions. While previously Damascus was able to focus its attention entirely upon the opening of the road to the sea, the accession of Ashurnazirpal now made the events in the north supreme in importance. For here Ashur, "the giant among the Semites," was concluding the overthrow of the Syrian states Bīt-Adini and Ḫattina and was getting into position to strike at Damascus in order to open up the road through Palestine. We may therefore surmise that Benhadad's coalition is in reality directed against Assyria, in view of the approaching peril. His purpose at Samaria is to coerce Ahab into the alliance, or else to cripple him so that he cannot aid Assyria. The siege of Samaria is thwarted, however, by the brilliant strategy of Ahab, who, under cover of a ruse, delivers a sudden attack on the surprised foe. The onslaught is carried right into the heart of the camp and Benhadad barely escapes by galloping off on the next best wagon horse (K H K 119). Naturally the army is dismayed. Turmoil ensues and a general rout follows. It was a glorious victory for Ahab and Israel and a disaster for Aram.

The Aramaeans, however, were not disposed to accept the verdict of this battle. Thus Benhadad in the following year again appeared upon the scene. This time Ahab was ready for him and faced him close to the border at the plain of Esdraelon. On the ranges south of the plain, perhaps in the vicinity of En Ğannīm, the Hebrews lay in two corps; poetically the narrative likens them to two herds of goats pasturing on a hillside. The Aramaeans, however, swarmed over the plain below, evidently waiting for the Israelites to descend into the valley, where the chariots could be used to better advantage. At length on the seventh day Ahab's chance came. He attacked the army of Benhadad and again won the day. The losses of the enemy were great (though the 100,000 of M T is preposterous). What remained of the Aramaean army fled to the nearby city of Aphek. The latter was taken by storm in a sanguinary battle. It was said that 27,000 Aramaeans lay buried beneath the razed walls (G V J 358). Benhadad himself was forced to surrender. Ahab received him with great kindness and generously allowed him to state his own peace terms.

These included the restitution of cities that had been taken from Israel and trade concessions in Damascus similar to those which Benhadad had obtained from Omri. They were accepted by the king of Israel and the Aramaean was allowed to go scot free.

CHAPTER VII

THE MESOPOTAMIAN KINGDOMS

In the century after the time of Tiglathpileser I the Aramaeans were able to form states in Mesopotamia without molestation from Ashur. In the extreme north in the region of the Tūr 'Abdīn lie the principalities of Shupria, north of the Tigris, and Nirdun to the south of it, while to the west in the vicinity of Diyarbekr is Bīt-Zamâni.[1] The latter state especially was a center of Aramaean influence. At the time of Ashurnazirpal its ruler Ammeba'la, a friend of the Assyrians, was slain by his nobles and a certain Bur-ramanu was raised to the throne. The Assyrian monarch, however, avenged the murder of his friend, flayed Bur-ramanu, and made Ilânu, a brother of Ammeba'la, king. But the latter also revolted, and so Ashurnazirpal was forced again to intervene in Bīt-Zamâni. In the same region the district of Zamua was also occupied by Aramaeans. Nûr-Adad the Sheikh of Dagara, with whom the monarch fought in the pass of Babit, rules over cities with clearly Aramaic names — Uzê, Birutu, Lagalaga. (Ann. Col. II 29.) But these localities lie apart from the great highway of progress and therefore do not interest us here. Of more importance are those states along the Euphrates and its tributaries. Opposite the mouth of the Ḫābûr, extending quite far downstream, the district of Suḫu, once held by the Amorites, was now Aramaean, and closely linked with it is a small principality of Ḫindân. North of the Euphrates, between it and the Ğebel Singār, lay the country of Laqê and within it the principality of Bīt-Ḫalupe (or Bīt-Ḫadippe(?) S A 107). Numerous independent city kingdoms also lay along the course of the Ḫābûr.

[1] Cf. Toffteen, Researches in Assyrian and Babylonian Geography, '08, p. 6 ff., on the cities of these regions.

The most powerful Aramaean state, however, was Bīt-Adini.[1] It occupied a strategic position on the great highway from Harran to Syria, and had as its capital Til-Barsip near the mouth of the Sağur on the right bank of the Euphrates south of Carchemish. This state extended west into Syria as far as the gates of Arpad [2] and in the east, towards Harran, the duchies Bīt-Baḫiani, Aṣalli, Tilabni, and Sarugi were its vassals.

The greater part of western Mesopotamia stood therefore under the influence of this powerful Aramaean state. Quite naturally Bīt-Adini sought to intrigue against Assyria; thus Ashurnazirpal tells that within the sphere of Assyria's influence, in Suru, the capital of Bīt-Ḫalupe,[3] identical with the present Sauar on the lower Ḫābûr (cf. A E T 176), a revolution had taken place 884 B.C. against the *shaknu* or custodian; the latter a Hamathite [4] was killed and "Aḫiababa, a man of unknown origin, whom they brought from Bīt-Adini they made their king" (Col. I 74f. A K A 281). Doubtless this revolution was instigated by Aḫuni and carried out under his auspices. Ashurnazirpal found it so important that he interrupted his campaign in Kummuḫ and marched down the Ḫābûr to Bīt-Ḫalupe, receiving on the way the Tribute of King Shulmān-ḫaman-ilāni of Sha-Dikanna [5] and of Ilu Adad of Qatni. When he reached Suru the elders and grandees came out and embraced his feet, saying, "If thou desirest slay! If thou desirest, let live!" It seems that the party loyal to Assyria

[1] The name must be derived from ʿadana = "dwell permanently," therefore a "settlement."

[2] In a geographical list (of later times, it is true), R T P 15, we have a list of some cities of Bīt Adini. Among them are Ḫaurani (Ḥawārīn near Yabrūd), Ḫazâzu (ʿAzāz), Nirabu (Nêrab near Aleppo) and the otherwise unknown towns Tuka, Saruna, Dinanu.

[3] Oppenheim, Der Tell Halaf, '08, p. 35, would identify this Tell, excavated by him, with Bīt-Ḫalupi. But this site, at the forks of the Ḫābūr, is too far north.

[4] This cannot mean the Hamath in Syria, but must refer to that in Mesopotamia mentioned by Tukulti-Ninib II (cf. the map in Scheil's Annales de Tukulti-Ninip, 1909).

[5] The identification of this city with the important site of ʿArbān remains the most probable, A E T 184.

was able to gain the upper hand and delivered up the rebels to Ashurnazirpal. On a pillar opposite the city gate he flayed all the ring-leaders or impaled them on stakes. Aḫiababa was brought to Nineveh and his skin spread out on the city wall. A loyal subject, Azi-ilu, was placed in charge of Bīt-Ḫalupe. The kings of the region of Laqê brought tribute, as did also Ḫaiân of Ḫindân; and Iluibni of Suḫu sent costly presents to Nineveh. In his third year, the Assyrian returning home from Naïri by way of the Tūr ʿAbdīn, received also the tribute of Aḫiramu, son of Yaḫiri ruler of Aṣalli and of Bît-Baḫianu which he describes as a "Hittite" land. (Col. II 22 f.) From the nature of these events we can readily divine that an anti-Assyrian confederacy was forming along the Ḫabûr under Bīt-Adini's help, and we see also that Ashurnazirpal was well alive to the danger and proceeded against it with vigor.

But it was not until some years later that the great Assyrian monarch was able to deal a decisive blow against these easterly states. The occasion presented itself in 879, when Babylon made the attempt to renew its claims in the middle Euphrates and leagued itself with Suḫu. Breaking up from his capital (Col. III 1 f) he marched in a wide half circle to Tabite[1] which lay southeast of Nisibis, perhaps at Tell Hamis and thence to the river Ḫarmish the modern Ğaghğagha (Z A XII 43), visiting Magarisi near the fork of this stream. The mountain of Iari in which the broken Obelisk locates this city must then be merely an abbreviation of Kashiari. The Harran Census (H C 39) mentions a city of Makrisu in "– –rê" (i.e., Iarê?) which is no doubt identical with our Magarisi. From Magarisi he descends to the Ḫābûr and exacts tribute from Sha-Dikanna. In his further progress down the river he stops at Qatni, perhaps identical with the great ruins of Shedāde (A E T 182), Shunaia, Dûr-katlime (ruins of Margada? cf. A E T 179),

[1] Its location is established by the Route of Tukulti Ninib, Annals Rev. 35. Coming up the Ḫābûr from Sha-Dikanna he passes Latiḫi, Duggaete, Magarisi, Guriete and then comes to Tabite. As Sachau has shown, Z A XII, 43, the name is preserved in the "equites sagittarii indigenae Thibithenses" who lay in garrison at Telbesmê (Notitia dignitatum, ed. Seeck, p. 78, no. 27).

Bīt-Ḫalupe (he refers doubtless to Suru-Sauar), and finally arrives opposite Sirqu. This city lay near the mouth of the Ḫābûr and on the right side of the Euphrates, as the annals of Tukulti Ninib prove. According to Ashurnazirpal III 134 it lay at the "crossing of the Euphrates." Scheil (48) compared the classical Circesium, but since the Aramaic name of the latter was Nabagath or Chabora that is impossible (Z A 27: 289). It seems to be a little too far south, otherwise it would be tempting to identify it with ancient Tirqa (Tell 'Ishar). From here he proceeds eastward over Ṣupri and Naqarabani[1] to the Euphrates, arriving opposite Ḫindân, the name of which Scheil (p. 44) has properly related to the classical Giddan on the left bank of the river. From here he marched to a mountain, which must mean the promontory opposite the tower of el Qayim, and after halting there continued on to Bīt-Garbaia (Bīt-Shabaia?)[2] opposite Ḫaridu, which may then be localized at Ğabarīya and Qal' at Rafida respectively. From Bīt-Garbaia the Assyrian proceeds to a point opposite Anat which has been correctly identified with the modern 'Ana and classical Anatho. (Z A 19:252.) Departing thence he storms the city of Ṡuru, whose name I hold may be preserved in the Wadi Sūr near Tilbesh. It was a stronghold of Shadudu, the ruler of Suḫi. Of the Babylonian contingent that aided Shadudu 50 troopers and 3000 men were captured; Shadudu with a small band, however, escaped across the Euphrates. After setting up his royal image in Suru the Assyrian returned to Calaḫ.

Shortly afterward (878?) Ashurnazirpal received the news of another rebellion in Laqê, Ḫindân, and Suḫu. He straightway goes to Suru on the Ḫābûr and orders ships to be built for his army. Meanwhile he marches to the mouth of the Ḫābûr and then eastward to the city of Ṣibate in Suḫu, destroying the towns

[1] Tukulti Ninib mentions between Sirqu and Ḫindān, Kasi, Arbate, Aqarbani (= Naqarabani) and Nagiate. Tukulti Ninib mentions east of Ḫindān, Kailite, Mashqite opposite Ḫarada .(= Ḫaridu) Anat, and Suri opposite Talbish (= the present Tilbesh).

[2] S A 103 identifies this place with the Beth-Garbaia of Ephraem Syrus, but this town must have been situated much further west.

of the region, reaping the harvests and slaughtering all defenders — 490 men. The main force of the Aramaeans had retired to the western side of the Euphrates and was intrenched at Ḫaridu. As his ships had now been completed, the monarch returned to the mouth of the Ḫābūr and ferried his army across the Euphrates. The allied forces of Suḫu, Laqê, and Ḫindân which advanced to meet him were defeated; 6500 men were killed and the remainder of the army perished in the desert from thirst. From Ḫaridu as far as Kipina the cities are sacked. In Kipina Azi-ilu of Laqê, doubtless identical with the Azi-ilu of Bīt-Ḫalupe, had intrenched himself. In the ensuing battle Ashurnazirpal killed 1000 men and carried off the booty and the gods of Kipina. Azilu, however, succeeded in retreating to the Bisuru mountains (the lesser Ǧebel il Bishri, near the mouth of the Balīḫ) some 100 km. above ed-Dēr. Dislodged from there he withdrew with heavy losses in rear guard actions undertaken to protect his herds, into Bīt-Adini to the border cities of Dummutu and Asmu.[1] The fact that he finds a haven of refuge in Bīt-Adini shows with sufficient clearness that the latter state was in sympathy with the rebels. Ashurnazirpal wreaked his vengeance on Dummutu and Asmu by burning them to the ground. He captured the rich herds of Azilu that were "innumerable as the stars of heaven" and apparently destroyed the remainder of the army, but the Aramaean chief himself escaped farther into Bīt-Adini. Meanwhile another Assyrian force had overcome Sheikh Ilâ of Laqê and captured his chariots and 500 of his men; these, together with the booty taken from Azi-ilu, are transported to Ashur by the victors. Another prince of Laqê, Ḫamti-ilu, who had taken refuge in his fortress, submitted and payed tribute. At the passes of the Euphrates the Assyrian founded two cities — Kar-Ashurnazirpal (Halebîyeh-Zenobia) and Nibarti-Ashur (Zalebiyeh-Chanuca) as outposts and bases against Bīt-Adini (Masp. III 30, A E T 164).

The struggle with these petty states on the lower Ḫābûr and its vicinity merely signified the warding off of the Aramaean peril

[1] In the modern Yāsim there may be a reminiscence of ancient Asmu.

from Assyria's own door. But the aims of the Assyrian monarch now went further. To safeguard the land against the Aramaeans it was necessary to strike at the heart of their power in Mesopotamia; and to lead Assyria on its path of destiny it was incumbent upon the monarch to follow in the footsteps of Tiglath-pileser I and open up the road to the western sea, which was blocked by Bīt-Adini. Therefore Ashurnazirpal directed his attention to the subjugation of this state. On the 20th of Sivan (June) he marched to Bīt-Adini. It is not clear whether this expedition followed the great road over Ras-el-'Ain and Harran, or whether it was undertaken from the newly founded cities at the passes of the Euphrates. The omission of the mention of Bīt-Baḫiani and Aṣalli speaks for the latter possibility. He approaches the border-fortress of Kaprabi (great rock!) a city "hanging like a cloud in the sky." Its people trusted in their strong garrison and did not come down to embrace his feet. At the command of the gods Ashur and Nergal he stormed and destroyed it, and deported 2400 of its troops to Calaḫ. After this feat of arms Aḫuni of Adini and Ḫabini of Til-Abni payed tribute and gave hostages.

Perhaps Ashurnazirpal vaingloriously believed that the terror of Assyria's military power had prostrated Aḫuni. Surely he did not appreciate the greatness of the Aramaean menace, else he would have completed the destruction of this foe, and would not have deported the Aramaeans to Calaḫ in numbers sufficient to endanger the national life of his own people. His ambitions, however, were primarily directed to obtaining control of Syria, wherefor on the 8th of Iyyar (868) he took the road to Carchemish. On the way he comes to Bīt Baḫiani, which pays tribute and furnishes a contingent of troops and chariots, then to Aṣalli, whose king Adad-'ime presents him with precious metals, chariots, horses, cattle, sheep and wine, then to Bīt-Adini, where he receives from Aḫuni costly articles of luxury, — ivory vessels, an ivory bed, an ivory throne overlaid with silver and gold, a dagger of gold, jewelry, live stock as well as a further number of troops.

Ḫabini of Tilabnâ [1] likewise appears with a tribute. On ships built of skins he crosses the Euphrates and comes to Carchemish, whose king Sangara (an Aramaean? cf. Hebrew Shamgar) pays a rich tribute including articles of ukarinnu wood, two hundred maidens, elephants' tusks, a gorgeous chariot and a couch of gold royally adorned. From Carchemish he then marches on into Syria (cf Ch. VIII). The submission of Carchemish and Bīt-Adini is peculiar. Possibly they were willing to have Ashurnazirpal overrun the Syrian states, especially Ḫattina, in order to profit by their weakness. Apparently also none of the Mesopotamian and Syrian states was prepared to combat the sudden and unexpected might of Assyria.

In 860 Shalmaneser came to the throne of Ashur. Aḫuni of Adini had by this time hastened preparations for combating Assyria and had begun to form a secret alliance against the great peril. One of the first acts of Shalmaneser was prophetic of his policy and showed his indorsement of his father's aims. For "he made shining" his weapons in the Mediterranean sea, sacrificed on its shores to his gods, and erected his image on the Lallar mountain in the Amanus. (Obelisk 276.) In his second year he marched to Bīt-Adini (Mon. I 29 f.). After crossing the Tigris he proceeded through the mountains of Ḫasamu [2] and Diḫnunu (the Nimrūd Dagh?) and reached the first city of Adini, — La'la'te, which must lie on the road Harran — Til Barsip. The inhabitants evacuated the town and fled into the mountains. After applying the torch to the place he advanced upon a fortress of Ki——qa (name mutilated). Aḫuni of Adini, "trusting in his numerous army," sallied out to meet him. By the help of the god Ashur the Assyrian succeeded in hurling his opponent back into the city, but refrained from attempting a siege. Instead, he proceeded to the unfortified town of Burmaruna, which he stormed, causing

[1] Tilabnâ is distinctly a more Aramaic form than Tilabni. The status emphaticus appears here unmistakably.

[2] I would identify this mountain with the Gebel abd-il-Aziz on whose western end is a village and ruins of Hossiwe, which may preserve the ancient name.

the slaughter of the small garrison of 300 men. Before the city he erected a pillar out of human heads. Burmaruna must have been situated on the Euphrates, where el-Burāt between Ğerabis and the mouth of the Sağur may mark its position. While at this city Ashurnazirpal received the tribute of Ḫabini of Tilabnâ Ga'uni of Sarugi and Giri-Adad of an unnamed principality. On ships of skins he next crossed the Euphrates, and after receiving the tribute of Kummuḫ he invaded Paqarruḫbuni, a province belonging to Adini and bordering on Gurgum. He defeated the Aramaeans at every point, burned their towns into ruins, filled the plain with their warriors' corpses, of which he counted 1300, and then marched on to Gurgum. His aim was to prevent the north Syrian states from giving succor to Adini, and to make ineffective the threatened coalition — a purpose achieved at the battles of Lutibu and Aliṣir (cf. Ch. VIII). For this reason perhaps he did not deal so thoroughly with Paqarruḫbuni and therefore even after the destruction of Bīt-Adini this region became the seat of another rebellion (848).

Shalmaneser's far-reaching policy had determined upon the annihilation of Bīt-Adini, and his manoeuvers in Syria, to be described in the next chapter, were primarily prompted by the desire of isolating this greatest enemy completely. On the 13th of Iyyar 858 he left Nineveh and marched to the capital of Aḫuni, Til-Barsip (Mon, II 13 f.). Aḫuni was defeated in battle on the left bank of the river and driven back across it to his city. The Assyrian also crossed over in the face of a freshet; but instead of besieging Til-Barsip, he attacked the western possessions of Aḫuni. Six fortresses, among them Sûrunu, Paripa, Til Bashiri (Tell Bashar), and Dabigu (Dābiq) were captured and spoiled and 200 other peaceful towns were sacked. He thus seems to have followed the Sağur and then turning about, proceeded down the Quwêq. Then, wheeling once more, he marched to the vicinity of Carchemish and assaulted Shazabê, which has been identified with the Syriac Shadabu, two parasangs below Ğerabis.[1] This city to-

[1] D P 68, and cf. Hoffmann, Auszüge aus den Syrischen Akten, etc., p. 164.

gether with the towns of its neighborhood, he burned into a ruined heap. His aim was clearly to intimidate the Hethitic states so that they should not render aid to Aḫuni. This strategy was effective, for the princes of the west paid tribute; — among them the kings of Sam'al, Ḫattina, Arpad, Carchemish, and Kummuḫ.

In the following summer, in the month of Tammuz 857, Shalmaneser again took the road to Til-Barsip to deal the finishing blow. But the adroit Aḫuni, in order to avoid certain annihilation, evacuated the capital and retreated with his army into Northern Syria. Shalmaneser was able to occupy the whole region of Bīt-Adini without resistance. The important cities of the land were made royal residences of the king of Assyria and received new names. Til-Barsip became Kâr-Shulmanasharid, Nappigu became Lita-Ashur, Aligu[1] became Aṣbat-la-kunu, Rugulitu became Qibit. . . . The cities of Pitru and Mutkinu on opposite sides of the Euphrates, which had been conquered by Tiglathpileser and under Ashur-irbe had been retaken by "the king of the land of Arumu," were restored again to Assyria and colonized anew. While delaying at Til-Barsip and organizing the new province,[2] Shalmaneser received the tribute of the kings of the seashore and of the Euphrates.

Kâr-Shulman-asharid, or Til-Barsip, has recently been discovered in the mound of Tell Aḥmār (P S B A '12, 66), situated near the mouth of the Sağur, and directly on the shore of the Euphrates, where there is an excellent ford. It therefore is south of Carchemish, and not north, as was formerly held (D P 263: Bireğīk). The country on this side of the river is flat for miles, but on the opposite side low and abrupt limestone hills come close to the river. The old ramparts of Til-Barsip, which warded off Shalmaneser, still stand. Within the wall a broken stela has been found,

[1] Nappigu has been identified with Membiğ (Hierapolis) south of the, Sağūr river. Aligu is compared with Leğah on the left bank of the Euphrates some distance above the mouth of the Sağūr.

[2] In the district of Til-Barsip lay also a city Kapridargilâ. The new cylinder of Sennacherib, C T XXVI col. VI 546, relates that S. found breccia for great stone vessels, such as had never before been found at this place.

representing an Assyrian king addressing a smaller male figure with conical cap and beard. It is doubtless Shalmaneser and his subject king. In the southeast gate which looks towards Nineveh, two basalt lions stood, bearing inscriptions of the Assyrian monarch. He calls himself: "the great king who hath swept the lands of Ḫatti, Guti and all the lands of the sun from the shore of the great sea of the setting sun, who hath defeated Muṣru and Urartu with its people, who hath swept the land of Ubu, the lands of Harutu and Labdadu, affecting their subjugation." These "mighty lions" were set up as symbols of victory in the "great gate of the city" after a triumph of Assyrian arms over some northern king who was in league with Urartu. In the midst of a great mountain the defeat was accomplished. Like a fierce windstorm that breaks the trees was Shalmaneser's onrush, and like the swoop of a hawk the attack of his troops.. The opposing king had to slink out of his camp as a thief in the night to escape.

In 856 (so the monolith II 66 f. while the black obelisk gives 854) Shalmaneser took up the pursuit of Aḫuni. The resourceful and courageous Aramaean had taken refuge in an almost impregnable citadel on a cliff "that hung down like a cloud from the sky" beside the Euphrates and which was called Shitamrat. It lay in an almost impassable region, a three days' journey from Til-Barsip. Shalmaneser boasts that none of his forefathers had ever penetrated thither. Aḫuni met the Assyrian in open battle, but was driven back into the city. The heads of his warriors were cut off and the mountain stained with the blood of his fighting men. The remnant of the army retreated to the top of the mountain. If Shalmaneser says that in the midst of the city a great battle ensued (Mon. II 73), we must refer this to the town below the acropolis. Elsewhere he relates that like the divine storm-bird his warriors attacked and killed 17,500 foemen (Balawat III, 3 f). He was unable to take the citadel itself by storm. Aḫuni, however, wisely chose not to subject his people to the privation of a long siege, but instead submitted and saved his and his people's lives. His treasure of incalculable weight, his troops and chariots and cavalry he surrendered to Shalmaneser. He himself, with his gods and sons and daughters and people, was deported to the vicinity of Ashur. The mere fact that he was not cruelly executed shows that his surrender took place while yet unconquered. Nevertheless, the state of Bīt-Adini was now a thing of the past, and its last hope of a revival removed.

The tragic end of the most powerful Aramaean state in the north is reflected in the prophecy of Amos 1:5: "I will exterminate the inhabitants of Biq'at Aven and the staff-holder" of Beth Eden (= Bīt-Adini).[1] The last shepherd of the pastoral people of Bīt-Adini shall perish. At the time when Amos prophesied, about 760 B.C. and after, Bīt-Adini was merely a geographical concept and no longer existed as a state, so that the translation "Scepter bearer" would be impossible. The disastrous deletion of this people is also played upon in the words of Sennacheribs Rabshaqeh (Is. 37:12, 2 Kings. 19:12): "Have the gods of the peoples that my fathers destroyed delivered them — Gozan[2] and Harran and Reseph[3] and the people of Eden (that dwell) at Telassar?" The latter name need not be amended into Tel-bashar (Winckler), but is rather the equivalent of Til-Ashûri. Essarhaddon (col. II 22) calls himself the one "who threshes the land of Barnaqi, the dwellers of the land of Til-Ashûri, which the people of Meḫranu call Mitanu.[4] Tiglathpileser I mentions a country of Mitani near the city of Araziqi (VI 61 f.), but it seems that we must seek

[1] Both names are often taken as appellatives, "valley of opulency" and "house of lust" (cf. Haupt, O L Z '10, 306) and referred to Damascus. But the first expression I hold to refer to the rich and fertile Biqâ' (Damascus can scarcely be called a "cleft"). Then Beth-Eden must also be a real geographical name. — My translation "staff-holder" I think is preferable to "*Stammhalter*," i.e., one who maintains the family descent, S A 77.

[2] Assyrian Guzana, the region at the forks of the Ḫābûr and the classical Gauzanitis.

[3] Assyrian Raṣappa, today Ruṣāfe (A E T 136). It seems to have become an Assyrian province as early as the time of Ashurnazirpal. Raṣappa means "paved street."

[4] Written Pi-ta-nu. The reading Mitanu suggested by Winckler, S B A '88: 1335, is accepted also by Toffteen, p. 13, and Jensen, *l.c.*

the Mitanu of Essarhaddon further north. For the location of Til-Ashûri is definitely fixed by Tiglathpileser I (Ann 176 f.), who mentions among its cities a number that can be fixed as lying west of the Kashiar mountains and the region of Bīt-Zamâni (cf. Toffteen 12 f.). The name Barnaqi may then survive in the Pornaki S. E. of Diyar-Bekr (Sachau 435) as Tomkins suggested. Meḫranu must be identical with the Maḫiranu of the Broken Obelisk (VI 19 A K A 136). Jensen identified it with the famous Tell Maḫre north of Ṛaqqā (Z A VI 58), while Tomkins compared Tell-el Meghrun S E of Harran (Sachau 227). It may be, however, that a more northerly location is necessary. Eden, then, in Isaiah is used in a wider sense than the name of the old state Bīt-Adini. And Telassar also appears to be a broad term, since it has survived in the ancient name of Mar'ash — Telesaura. The mention of Eden (Ezek. 27:23) alongside of Harran and Calneh must have in mind the city of Til-Barsip, which no doubt remained a great center of commerce at all times.

Concerning the smaller Aramaean principalities of Mesopotamia little remains to be said. In 854 Shalmaneser advanced against Giammu, king of the Balīḫ region, north of Harran, who was evidently rebelling (Mon. II 78 f.). Frightened by his advance, the Aramaeans of the district assassinated their king and opened their cities to Shalmaneser. The monarch entered Kitlala and Til-sha-turaḫi, introduced Assyrian gods, held a feast in Giammu's palaces, and spoiled his treasure. From here he went directly to Til-Barsip and into Syria (cf. Ch. VIII). In the following year he conquers Til-abnê (Obelisk 67 f.). The capital and near-by towns are taken, but the king Ha——rat seems to have escaped. Since from here he goes up to the source of the Tigris to erect his image in the Subnatgrotto (Sebeneh-Su) and sacrifice to the gods, I am disposed to find Tilabni not at Urfa, as does Maspero (III 31), but south of the Karağah Dagh, at Tela (Viranshehir) or the near-by Tell Anabi.[1] Henceforth the Mesopotamian Aramaeans offer no resistance.

[1] Tell Halaf might also claim consideration.

CHAPTER VIII

THE NORTH SYRIAN STATES

In that part of Syria north of the 36th parallel we find a number of states of mixed Hittite, Canaanite, and Aramaean character and possessing a relatively high civilization. The northernmost of these is Gurgum, which in part belongs to the sphere of Asia Minor. This state, it seems, was affected by the Aramaean migration earlier than the others, for its name is Aramaic and means "the hard pit of the pomegranate" (S B A 92:314). Nevertheless its kings down to very late days bear Hittite names, so that it would seem that the Aramaeans could not hold themselves against the great pressure of the Asia Minor peoples. The capital of Gurgum was at Marqasi (to-day Marʿash *l. c.* 318) and owed its prominence to its strategical position on one of the main highways into Cilicia. Gurgum had as its southerly neighbor Sam'al, the capital city of which was Senğirli. The excavations at this site have revealed the existence of a culture which sprang up after the fourteenth century under Hittite rule. The city commanded the Amanus Pass that leads to the coast, and already at the beginning of the period of fortification it was a great stronghold. Sam'al is described as lying "at the foot of the Amanus," and it extended south about as far as the latitude of Killiz. Here it bordered on the state of Ḫattina, whose center was the ʿAmq of the lake of Antioch and which in the north controlled the district circumscribed by the Aleppo-Iskenderûn highway and on the left side of the Orontes extended down to the Nahr il-Kebir. Its capital was at Kunalua (Kunalia, Kinalia). To the east the state of Yaḫan with the capital Arpad (Tell Erfâd) and the principality of Ḫalman (Aleppo), a great sanctuary of the god Hadad, bordered on Ḫattina. South of Ḫattina and Aleppo begins the country of Hamath, which belongs, however, to the zone of Central Syria.

After intimidating the Mesopotamian Aramaeans, Ashurnazirpal (876 B.C.) took up the march to the sea (A K A 367). The most natural outlet for Assyria's trade and traffic with the seaboard of the Mediterranean was the highway to the gulf of Alexandrette. This road passed directly through the state of Ḫattina, whose subjugation was therefore a political necessity. From Carchemish the Assyrian passed into Syria between the mountains Munzigani and Ḫamurga (identical perhaps with the valley of Shekib east of the Quwêq river in the latitude of Killiz), leaving the land of Aḫanu (= Yaḫan) to the left, and reached the first city of Ḫattina, — Ḫazaz, long since identified with the modern 'Azāz S. W. of Killiz. He explicitly states that he avoided Yaḫan; the cause of this regard for its neutrality may be found in the aim of Ashurnazirpal to reach Ḫattina without delay. At Ḫazaz he received gold, linen garments, and other goods as tribute. From here he marched eastward to the Aprê (Afrīn) river, and after crossing it, doubtless at the point where the Aleppo-Iskenderûn road still crosses it, near iz-Ziyadiyeh, he called a halt. Breaking camp again, he approached Kunalua, the capital of Ḫattina, which is perhaps preserved in Tell Kunana (Tomkins, Bab. Or. Rec. III 6). Ashurnazirpal relates that king Lubarna of Ḫattina submitted in terror and payed a heavy tribute, viz. 20 talents of silver, 1 talent of gold, 100 talents of lead, 100 talents of iron, 1000 head of cattle, 10,000 sheep, 1000 brightly colored garments, cloth, a couch of ukarinnu wood sumptuously inlaid, dishes of ivory and ukarinnu wood beyond estimate, female musicians, a great kû-monkey and great birds (ostriches? — Textb. 16 and A K A 369). In addition, the Assyrian levied troops from Lubarna and took hostages from him. While he was at Kunalua he received the tribute of King Gusi of Yaḫan.

From Kunalua the Assyrian marched through the 'Amq, apparently recrossing the Afrīn near the lake of Antioch, and reached the Orontes.[1] The latter he must have crossed south of it-Tlēl Baḫshīn. For immediately afterward he passes between the mountains Yaraqu and Ya'turu, which have been aptly identified with the Ğebel Qoṣeir, and then crosses another mountain (Ashtama?) - ku (Maspero II 40). He therefore goes through the notch of the Qoṣeir over Qyzylğa and Bāwerā, and then over the Ğebel Shahsīm at Beled-ish-Sheikh. Thereupon he arrives at the Sagur (or Sangur) river, which must be the Nahr il-Kebīr[2] and can scarcely be the il Abyaḍ (M V A G '02, 2, 61), seemingly near the point where the road to Laodicea crosses it to-day. It has been suggested that in Ğishr-*esh-Shughr*, where the Laodicea road leaves the Orontes, the name Sagur is still preserved. Since the river Sağūr near Carchemish has the same name, both of them must have been christened by the early Hittites. After resting at the il Kebīr, Ashurnazirpal passed between the mountains of Saratini and Duppani, which must consequently be found in the northern Bargylus in the Ğebel Daryūs, and then halted again at the *shore of the sea?* (Textb. p. 16). From here he came to Aribua, a fortress belonging to Lubarna of Ḫattina, which is doubtless the present Qala'at il Arba'in (M V A G '02, 2, 61) at a strategical point, where the states of Ḫattina, Hamath, and Arvad bordered on one another.[3] Aribua is occupied by Ashurnazirpal and the grain of the land of Luḫuti is harvested and stored away. The fortress becomes an Assyrian stronghold with a military garrison, and is consecrated to this purpose in an especial festival. While his headquarters were at Aribua, the Assyrian brought about a great slaughter in Luḫuti, sacking the towns and hanging all captives

[1] Dussaud, R A '08, 277. Winckler supposed (A O F I 5) that the Assyrian marched around the north side of the lake of Antioch, crossed the Orontes near the sea and passed by the Mons Casius (G. il Aqra), which he identifies with Mt. Yaraqu. But it seems to me that then the crossing of the Kara-Su ought to have been mentioned. A second crossing of the Afrīn need not be recorded.

[2] Hommel, Geschichte, 581; Delattre, L'Asie Occidentale, 496.

[3] Dussaud, R A '08, 228, and Maspero, III 40, go too far south. I cannot convince myself that Lubarna's power extended any further south than the zone of Gebal-Apamea. There Hamath's sphere of interest began.

in sight of their burning villages. This conduct is indeed strange, since Lubarna had submitted and since Aribua was occupied without resistance. We are therefore led to suppose that Aribua did not lie in Luḫuti, but only on the edge of it. On the other hand Luḫuti can be no independent state, for neither a king nor a capital is mentioned. And if it be merely a province, then it must belong to Hamath, and be identical with the La'ash of the Zakir inscription (cf. Ch. XI). Ashurnazirpal is therefore striking at Hamath's left flank with the dual purpose of gaining a hold on the Emesa-Tripolis highway, and of intimidating the Phoenician cities. Both aims are achieved. For from Luḫuti he reaches the northern edge of the Lebanon and follows it to the sea to Tripolis,[1] where he purifies his weapons and sacrifices to the great gods. And at this point he then receives the tribute of the Phoenician cities from Tyre north to Arvad; it does not seem to have been a large tribute, however, since he neglects to give us a detailed summary. The proud cities of the seaboard in no way humiliated themselves, and it is thus only a vain boast if the Assyrian tells that they embraced his feet. Hamath seems to have paid no attention to the invasion of its western province, and certainly did not pay tribute. From Tripolis Ashurnazirpal returned to Nineveh, visiting the Amanus mountains en route to erect a stela of himself, to sacrifice to the gods and to cut the precious timbers needed for the Temple of Sin and Shamash. His expedition had opened the roads to the sea at three points — Iskenderûn, Laodicea, and Tripolis. A strong foothold in Syria had indeed been gained.

The accession of Shalmaneser found the Syrian states preparing for a united resistance against Assyrian claims and ambitions. Bīt-Adini, realizing how desperate was its position, succeeded in leaguing to itself Ḫattina, Carchemish, Gurgum and Sam'al. Shalmaneser's plan of campaign provided for the putting down

[1] Hence Luḫuti extends from the vicinity of Qal'at il Arba'in to the Tripolis highway. It includes the greater part of the Bargylus and is therefore larger than Dussaud, R.A '08, p. 228, and Maspero, III 40, suppose.

of the rebellion in the west first of all, in order to maintain what his father had achieved in Syria, and to strike at the coalition before it had time to prepare fully. In his second year he crossed the Euphrates and began to roll up the coalition from the north (Mon. col. I 36 f.). Kummuḫ paid tribute straightway and thus withdrew from the alliance. Shalmaneser, therefore, advanced first against Gurgum, whose king Mutallu, perhaps owing to the perfidy of Kummuḫ its neighbor, also submitted. From Gurgum the Assyrian turned to Sam'al. Ḫani of Sam'al offered resistance in his fortress of Lutibu, aided by detachments of troops sent by his allies — Ahuni of Bīt-Adini, Sapalulme of Ḫattina and Sangar of Carchmish. Near Lutibu[1] the Hittite-Aramaean coalition gives battle. Shalmaneser claims the victory and says that he stained the mountain with the blood of his foe, but it seems to have been won with difficulty; he had to implore the aid of Nergal and Ashur during the fight. Ḫani's forces retreat into the fortress in safety and are left unmolested. The Assyrian merely erects a pillar of human heads opposite Lutibu, destroys some defenseless towns, and erects a mighty image of himself with an account of his heroism, at the source of the Saluara river.[2]

It is scarcely possible that the allied kings were present in person at Lutibu. For Shalmaneser marches south alongside the foot of the Amanus, and, skirting the lake of Antioch, crosses the Orontes river into Ḫattina, where he again meets the same kings at Aliṣir. If, after the defeat at Lutibu, they had retreated such a great distance, the Assyrian would have certainly pursued them. On the other hand Hâni of Sam'al is represented as having

[1] There is a possibility that Lutibu may be only a by-name of Sam'al (Senǧirli), for the fighting must have taken place in this immediate vicinity, as S B A 92: 335 also holds. The great strength of the Senǧirli citadel would make Shalmaneser's withdrawal without besieging it comprehensible. It may be preferable, however, to identify Lutibu with Saktshegözü 25 km. N.E. of Senǧirli. Cf. on this site and its remains O L Z '09: 377.

[2] The Aramaic name means "Eel" river. The stream is identical with the modern Kara-Su. The old name, however, is still preserved in the village of Sulmara near its source. S B A '92: 330.

been bottled up in Lutibu, and now appears again in Ḫattina. The matter is still further complicated by the fact that the coalition is augmented by the kings of Que, Cilicia and Yasbiqu (cf. Ishbak Gen. 25:2). How these forces could arrive so speedily in Ḫattina is extremely obscure, unless they came to the mouth of the Orontes by ships from Tarsus. We are thus confronted by two possibilities; either Shalmaneser after the battle of Lutibu was engaged in other unmentioned operations further east, and so gave the allies from Asia Minor and Syria time to assemble at the border of Ḫattina, or else he is chronicling inexactly when he states that Ḫâni was present at Aliṣir and the others participated at Lutibu.

The border fortress of Aliṣir, which must have been situated at Antioch or in its vicinity, was taken after a hard battle. With his own hand Shalmaneser captured Buranate, King of Yasbuqu. From Aliṣir he approached the great cities of the king of Ḫattina; the upper ones of Amurrû and the sea of the setting sun he overthrew like a wave of the deluge. Along the wide coast of the sea he marched, receiving the tribute of the kings of the seaboard. All his operations were thus conducted in the Bargylus region. His statements, however, are so vague and his neglect to mention further what became of the hostile coalition so peculiar, that it would seem that he suffered a serious reverse somewhere in the mountains. At any rate he soon wheeled about and returned to the Amanus. At the mountain of Atalur (also called Lallâr, "mountain of honey" S A 58), which is the promontory of Rhosus north of the mouth of the Orontes (P S B A '15, 229), where Ashurirbe of old had erected his royal statue, Shalmeneser set up his own image. Then he turned homeward, conquering on his way the cities of Taiâ, Ḫazâzu, Nulia and Butamu[1] in Ḫattina, killing 2800 warriors and carrying off large booty. Arame of Gusi (Arpad), who had not joined the alliance against Assyria, paid tribute.

[1] The site of Ḫazaz being known (ʿAzāz), we may look for Taiâ to the west and Nulia and Butamu to the east, between ʿAzāz and Dābiq. The Assyrians are bound for Til-Barsip. Nulia I think may be the modern Niyara. Butamu Tomkins (*l.c.*, p. 6) aptly compared to Beitān near ʿAzāz.

In the following year (858) Shalmaneser attacked the cities of Bīt-Adini west of the Euphrates and came very close to the border of Ḫattina at Dabigu (to-day Dābiq Z A XII 47). The kings of Syria, chastened by the events of the previous season, brought him tribute. The Ḫattinaean paid the sumptuous amount of 3 talents of gold, 100 talents of silver, 300 talents of iron, 100 copper vessels, 1000 brightly colored and linen garments, his daughter and her rich dowry, 20 talents of bright purple, 500 head of cattle, 5000 sheep. Besides this Shalmaneser imposed upon him a yearly tax, to be delivered at Ashur, of 10 talents of silver, 2 talents of purple, and 200 cedar beams. The tribute imposed on Sangar of Carchemish is a close second in rank. It included 3 talents of gold, 70 talents of silver, 30 talents of bronze, 100 talents of iron, 20 talents of bright purple, 500 weapons, his daughter and her dowry, 100 daughters of his nobles, 500 head of cattle, 5000 sheep; his yearly tax was fixed at 1 mina of gold, 1 talent of silver, 2 talents of purple. Ḫaiâni, son of Gabbar, "from the foot of the Amanus," who is doubtless identical with Ḫani of Sam'al, brought 10 talents of silver, 90 talents of bronze, 20 talents of iron, 300 brightly colored and linen garments, 300 head of cattle, 3000 sheep, 2000 cedar beams, his daughter and her dowry, together with an annual tax of 10 minas of gold and 200 cedar beams. Arame, "son of Bīt-Agusi," gave 10 minas of gold, 6 talents of silver, 500 head of cattle, 5000 sheep; he appears to remain exempt from further taxation. Katazil of Kummuḫ agreed to a yearly tribute of 20 minas of silver and 300 cedar beams. From this it appears that Carchemish and Ḫattina were the richest states of northern Syria.

After Shalmaneser in the following years had accomplished the destruction of Bīt-Adini he at length in 854 turned his face westward. He is bound for the country of Hamath, bent upon new conquests in Central Syria. The kings of northern Syria — Sangar of Carchemish, Kundashpi of Kummuḫ, Arame son of Gusi, Lalli of Melid, Ḫaiâni, son of Gabbar, Kalparuda of Ḫattina, Kalparuda [1] of Gurgum acknowledged their vassalship by ap-

[1] Dittography of the previous name?

pearing before him at Pitru, and bringing tribute (Mon. II 82 f.). From Pitru he marched to Ḫalman (Aleppo) which submitted in fear at his approach and paid silver and gold. Before leaving Ḫalman the monarch brought sacrifice to the god Hadad, who had a famed sanctuary in this city.

The attack upon central Syria, and especially the outcome of the battle of Qarqar, appears to have weakened the prestige of Shalmaneser. For after an expedition to the upper Tigris and two campaigns in Babylonia, he was forced to return to Syria. Perhaps Arpad and Carchemish refused to pay tribute, for in 850 he made a raid into the territory of both. In 848 he found it necessary to deport the restless population of Paqaraḫbuni (Ann. 85–91). In 832 finally we hear again of Ḫattina (Ann. 147 f.). While at Calaḫ, Shalmaneser is informed that the Hattinaeans have assassinated their king Lubarna (II) and have made Surri, who had no claim to the throne, their king. The Assyrian dispatches his war-chief Daiân Ashur, a remarkable general, to Kinalua, the capital of Ḫattina. The city is assaulted and sanguinary fighting ensues. Surri dies suddenly, — the Annals claim of fright. His son Zaipparma and other ringleaders of the rebellion are seized by the people, surrendered by them to Daiân Ashur and cruelly impaled. Sâsi, son of Kuruzza, of the loyal Assyrian party, is made king of Ḫattina. A large tribute is imposed and the image of Shalmaneser is erected in the temple of the gods at Kinalua. From now on the name Ḫattina disappears from the inscriptions. The power of this state is greatly reduced, and its realm confined to the ʻAmq of Antioch, so that it receives the name Unqi. The earliest occurrence of it is in the inscription of Zakir (cf. Ch. XI). Ḫattina's southern possessions in the Bargylus appear to have been lost to Hamath.

Northern Syria was from now on quite firmly under Assyria's control and isolated attempts at rebellion were suppressed without great difficulty.

CHAPTER IX

THE SUPREMACY OF DAMASCUS

THE Assyrians had succeeded in laying open the road to the sea. The next logical step was to safeguard this achievement from covetous neighbors. This required constant campaigns both in the north and in the south. In central Syria it was especially Damascus, with its ally Hamath, that threatened to contest Assyria's claims in the west. The conquest of these states, therefore, became a necessity for the new world-power. Furthermore, beyond Damascus there beckoned Tyre and Sidon, Palestine and South Arabia. To unite this great avenue of commerce from Asia Minor to Africa, under a common scepter, with all that such a thing implies, in coinage and language, law and order, was indeed a lofty aim, achieved for a passing moment by Esarhaddon, realized in the empire of the Persians.

In the year 854 Shalmaneser crossed the border of Ḫattina into Hamath. He approached first the cities of Adennu and Bargâ. The former has been suitably identified with Tell Dānīt, southeast of Idlib (R A '08, 225). Bargâ should then lie to the south of it, but close by — perhaps at Stūma. Adennu is called "Adâ, a city of Urḫileni of Hamath" on band IX of the gates of Balawat. It and Pargâ (or Bargâ) surrendered to the Assyrian. His first blow struck Arganâ, a royal city, which is perhaps identical with the modern Rīḥā on the north side of the mountain of the same name (R A '08, 225).[1] The city was captured and pillaged, and the palaces of king Irḫuleni of Hamath were set in flames. From here the Assyrian marched to Qarqar, the ancient Apamea and modern Qalʻatil Mudîq (Masp. III 70). At Qarqar a great

[1] Is the name, as Dussaud supposes, preserved in the swamp of ir-Rūǧ further west?

battle is fought with twelve kings of Syria, of whom only eleven, however, are specified.

This Syrian league is composed of Adad-idri of Damascus, Irḫuleni of Hamath, Ahab of Israel, the king of Irkana, and Adunuba'li of Shiana. But Que, Muṣri, Arvad, Ushana, Ammon, and an Arabian tribe are also represented. Damascus furnishes 1200 chariots, 1200 horsemen, and 20,000 men infantry. Israel lends 2000 chariots and 10,000 men. Hamath is third, with 700 chariots, 700 horsemen, and 10,000 men. Irkana and Shiana each furnish 10,000 men, but only 10 and 30 chariots respectively. Muṣri is represented by 1000 men, Que by 500, and Ushana and Arvad (under its king Matinuba'li) each by 200. The cavalry is strongly reënforced by the 1000 camels of Gindibu the Arabian. Ba'sa mâr Ruḫubi of Ammon finally had at least a thousand men in his detachment.

As usual Shalmaneser claims the victory in extravagant phrases. Thus the monolith (II 96 f.) relates: "With the exalted power that the Lord Ashur granted, with the mighty weapons that Nergal who goes before me, presented, I fought with them, from Qarqar to Gilzâu I accomplished their defeat. Fourteen thousand of their warriors I prostrated with weapons, like Hadad I caused the storm to rain upon them, heaped up their corpses, filled the surface of the field. Their numerous troops with the weapons I slew, their blood I made flow over the expanse of the plain. Too small was the field for the slaughter, the wide plain did not suffice to bury them. With their corpses I dammed the Orontes as with a bridge. In the midst of that battle I took their chariots, riders, horses, and harnesses."

Shalmaneser has bequeathed us also several other versions of this great battle. According to the Annals(66) 20,500 foemen are slain, a Bull inscription from Nimrūd gives 25,000, a recent statue from Ashur 29,000. But even the more conservative figure of the monolith — 14,000 — must be regarded as greatly exaggerated. In a certain sense the battle was an Assyrian victory, since Shalmaneser remained master of the field, whereas the allies retreated. But at Gilzâu, which may be the Seleucid Larissa (Qal'at Seğar),[1] they again halted. Directly on the bank of the Orontes, which here runs through a steep and narrow valley, the battle raged. Shalmaneser boasts that he dammed the river with the corpses of his foes, but in reality he must have suffered a defeat at this citadel. Had he been victorious he would surely have pressed on to Hamath. Thus success at Qarqar and failure at Gilzâu attend his first campaign against the Syrian league.

When we compare this account of the cuneiform inscriptions with our Old Testament narrative, the difficulty of harmonizing them becomes vexing. As we have seen, Ahab of Israel fought successfully against Damascus, and even captured its king at Aphek, making of him a vassal. The Hebrew account deserves full credence, the more since Ahab is distasteful to the prophetic narrators, so that an exaggeraton of his deeds would not have been allowed to pass into our record unchallenged. If this tradition is discarded and Ahab made the vassal of Benhadad (Winckler), such procedure is utterly arbitrary.

The difficulties increase when we regard the name of Ahab's opponent in the Old Testament and of his suzerain in the inscriptions of Shalmaneser. Where the Bible reads Benhadad the Assyrian gives (ilu) IM-idri. The fact that the LXX translates Benhadad by "son of Ader" led to the supposition that *hādār*, "glory," and not the divinity Hadad was originally the second element of this name. It would have been more natural to conclude, however, that hādār was a later modification of Hadad for the purpose of avoiding the name of this heathen divinity. It was furthermore supposed that the ideogram I M could be read "Bir," and that Bir was an Aramaean divinity. Thus Birhadar was held by many to be the original name rather than Barhadad.[2]

[1] Here the retreat from Qarqar would most logically reach the Orontes. For a description of the place cf. Bell, The Desert and the Sown, p. 235.

[2] Cf. A T U 73 and most recently Zimmern in the Hilprecht Anniversary Volume, p. 303. The name Barhadad occurs in Christian days as that of a bishop in Mesopotamia; cf. von Gutschmid, Neue Beiträge zur Geschichte des Alten Orients, 46 f.

But, admittedly, the existence of a god Bir is not established by indisputable evidence (K A T 446) and, admittedly, the ideogram (ilu) IM is regularly the equivalent of Adad. And in the god-lists we are explicitly told that Addu and Dadu were the names of the god IM in Amurrū (C T XXV pl. 16:16). For this reason Adad-idri is the only possible reading of this name, and its only possible form in Hebrew could be Hadadezer (A J S L 27:27 f.). Benhadad and Hadadezer cannot be identified except under the theory that the full name was Ben-Hadadezer, of which the Assyrians dropped the first element and the Hebrews the last. In addition to the fact that this name is of a most improbable formation, this theory is full of difficulties.[1]

Luckenbill has shown one way out of the dilemma by the assertion that Benhadad is not identical with Adad-idri, but rather the latter's predecessor (A J S L 27:277 f.). Then the fighting between Ahab and Benhadad might possibly have taken place about 860. The change of rulers at Tyre, where Pygmalion (860–814) came to the throne, may have been the signal for Benhadad to attack Ahab, since the latter could now expect no help from his ally. The battle of Aphek, then, took place in 859, whereupon two years of peace with Aram followed.[2] The death of Benhadad took place, no doubt, during this interim in 858 and Adad-idri became king in Damascus. Possibly he was a usurper, most certainly he was a vigorous and able ruler. In 857–856 he made war upon Israel and gained Ramoth in Gilead from the Hebrews. Ahab can have suffered no crushing defeat, for then he would not have had the superiority in chariots with which he is credited by Shalmaneser. It is probable that in view of the common danger from Assyria, Ahab, who appears as a wise statesman, made peace with Adadidri and then in 854 appeared as the latter's ally at the battle of Qarqar. Perhaps believing the danger from Assyria to be over for the present, Ahab in the following year was led to undertake the campaign against the Aramaeans to

[1] Cf. Zeitschrift für Keilschriftforschung, II, 167.

[2] These L. unnecessarily assigns to the years after Qarqar, *l.c.*, 279.

reconquer Ramoth Gilead in which he met his fate. It must be noted that in this account (1 Kings 22) the opponent of Ahab is not mentioned by name, as in the preceding chapter, but is merely called "King of Aram." (Luckenbill, p. 281.) It is perfectly possible to assume, therefore, that a period of five or six years intervenes between 1 Kings 20 and 22 and that the "King of Aram" is our Adad-idri. We can now also account for the fact that the king of Israel does not appear among Shalmaneser's foes again after 854, because the new king Joram (853–842) was engaged in unsuccessful attempts to subdue the rebellious Moab (2 Kings 3).[1]

The result of Qarqar was not discouraging to the Syrians. Indeed, after settling more urgent business in Babylonia, Shalmaneser returned in 850 to Syria and found also Arpad and Carchemish rebellious. According to the Bull inscription he crossed the Euphrates for the eighth time and burned and destroyed many cities belonging to Sangar of Carchemish, captured Arne,[2] a royal city of Arame of Arpad and sacked it, together with 100 towns of its neighborhood. This campaign, according to the Black Obelisk (85–86), took him all that year. The Bull inscription is mistaken in assuming an attack on the Syrian league in that season (Textb. 21). It must also be mistaken in repeating the incursion into Carchemish and Arpad, where 97 and 100 cities respectively are sacked. The 100 cities of Arpad could scarcely be destroyed twice in succession. His trip to the Amanus, however, must belong

[1] If our modification of the Luckenbill theory gives a rational explanation of the problems confronting us, then we must conclude that 2 Kings 8: 7–15 is, to say the least, inaccurate when it makes Hazael the successor of Benhadad. Either we must suppose Benhadad to be an error for Adadidri in vss. 7, 9 (or a gloss!) or else deny the passage as unhistorical, for which there is hardly enough ground (G V J 365). Those who would abide by the text must take recourse to Kittel's theory (*ibid.* 359 ff.) that Shalmaneser is in error when he mentions Ahab as his opponent, and that Ahab died 855, so that his son Joram fought at Qarqar. Then the battle of Aphek took place 858. Under this supposition the Benhadad-Adadidri problem, however, remains unsolved.

[2] Band XII of the gates of Balawat records also the capture of ". . . agdâ, a city of Arame son of Gusi."

to the 11th year, although it is not mentioned by the Obelisk (87–89), according to which he captures 89 towns of Hatti and Hamath. Traversing the Yaraqu mountains, apparently in the footsteps of Ashurnazirpal, he reached the cities of Hamath in the Bargylus. Here he captured the important place of Ashtamaku, as well as 97 towns of the region, bringing about great slaughter. At this time, the Bull inscription vaguely tells, Adad-idri, Irḫuleni, and twelve other (?) kings of the seaboard went forth to meet him. He claims to have accomplished their defeat, slain 10,000 of their warriors, and taken away their weapons, chariots, and horses. It is impossible to say where the battle took place. On his return he went to the Amanus for cedars, and then back to Mesopotamia. On the way he captured Apparasu, a fortress in Arpad (perhaps to-day Taṭmarāsh, northwest of Erfād) and received the tribute of King Kalparundi[1] of Ḫattina. In 848 he found it necessary to undertake a punitive expedition against Paqarḫubuna (the territory of Bīt-Adini west of the Euphrates) as we learn from the Black Obelisk (896).

In 846, his 14th year, Shalmaneser makes a supreme effort. He mobilizes troops from all parts of his domain, as the Bull inscription informs us, and with 120,000 men crosses the Euphrates. The same Syrian league (this time 14 kings) again takes the field against him. At Qarqar about 60,000 men had fought against Shalmaneser. But now the huge army of the Assyrian must have necessitated a much greater levy. Shalmaneser claims that he routed the enemy; but since he furnishes no facts at all, we must regard his statement with distrust. During the next three years he was busy with operations in Nairi, Namri, and the Amanus.

About this time a change of rulers took place at Damascus.

[1] Apparently the last king of this state. Sachau, Z A 6: 432, has shown that the name occurs in an Aramaic inscription of the seventh century, C I S II no. 75, "To Akrabu (?) son of Gabbarud, the eunuch, who drew near unto Hadad." Gal-pa-ru-da, Galpurundi, Garparunda, Gabbarud are all variations of the same name. The one of this inscription may have been a Syrian prince whose son suffered the fate referred to in Is. 39: 7.

Concerning this event an Ashur text (M K A no. 30:25) says, "Adad-idri forsook the land (i.e. died); Hazael, son of a nobody seized the throne." More detailed information is presented in 2 Kings 8:7–15, if we delete the name Benhadad as a gloss and refer "king of Aram" to Adad-idri. According to this passage Elisha reads the mind of Hazael, who has been sent to him by the king, and recognizes his innermost ambitions and designs. Alone with the King in his chamber soon afterward, Hazael smothers him with a wet blanket (so that no sign of murder can be detected) and then, with the help of other conspirators, seizes the throne of Damascus.

Adadidri must have been an able and a brilliant ruler. With his death the Syrian league seems to have fallen apart. Assyrian diplomacy may have speeded this. Concerning Israel we know that Joram asserted his independence by emphasizing his claims on Gilead (2 Kings 8:28). He attacked Ramoth, captured it, and then "held the watch" against Hazael, king of Aram (9:14) and after being wounded, went to Jezreel for a rest-cure. With his murder by Jehu, the dynasty of Omri reaches its end. Hazael meanwhile was laboring under great difficulties, and needed time to whip his vassals back into line. But Shalmaneser, seeing his advantage, was quick to make use of it.

In 842, therefore, he advanced upon Damascus without tarrying on the way. Hamath must have submitted and allowed him to pass on unmolested. At the mountain of Saniru (the Shenir of Deut. 3:9), "in front of the Lebanon," Hazael intrenched himself. The "Lebanon" must here refer to the Antilebanon range, before whose southern "front" the Saniru or Hermon, lies (Textb. 24). Of course, the Assyrian does not mean to say that Hazael intrenched himself on the top of the great Hermon! Haupt thinks the Ğebel ez-Zebedānī, 50 km. northwest of Damascus, is meant (Z D M G 69:169). Most assuredly the position which the Aramaean took was in the close vicinity of the Wadi Zerzer on the present railroad from Damascus to Shtōrā, for the Assyrians must have approached Damascus from the Biqâʻ on the very same route as does the modern traveller coming from Bērūt. In the ensuing battle Hazael was forced to retreat to Damascus. Besides the slaughter of 6000 Aramaeans, Shalmaneser claims a large booty of 1121 chariots, 470 riding horses, and Hazael's camp. But this battle had evidently cost him so heavily that he was unable to lay siege to Damascus. He had to content himself with destroying the beautiful parks of the vicinity and with a raid against defenseless towns in the Hauran. Then he turned back to the Phoenician coast, journeying as far as the mountains of Ba'li-ra'-si (the promontory at the Nahr-el-Kelb above Bērūt), where he set up his royal image, which is still standing to-day.[1] Here he received the tribute of Tyre, Sidon and Jehu of Israel. This fact is of extreme importance. None of these states needed to pay tribute. Arvad, Simyra and Ushana were much nearer and yet did not find it necessary. The significance of the act is twofold. We see first that Jehu maintains the tradition of the house of Omri of fraternizing with Sidon and Tyre (cf. the words of the disappointed prophetic writer 2 Kings. 10:31). And furthermore we perceive that these three states make a bid for Assyrian friendship and thereby declare themselves the foes of Aram. For Israel's history it was a momentous decision.

Under this aspect, the attitude of Hazael, that Elisha foresaw, becomes perfectly clear. He is filled with an implacable hatred for Israel. True, for the present he could not pay any attention to this southern neighbor, for his mind and strength were occupied with the Assyrian menace. In 839 Shalmaneser made a last attempt to strike at Damascus. The Obelisk (102–4) tells that he captured four of the Aramaean's cities, and received the tribute of Tyre, Sidon, and Gebal. The eponym chronicle designates the campaign for this year as "to the land of Danabi." This can only refer to the classical Danaba and the Dunip of the Amarna letters, which lay perhaps at Ṣednāyā north of Damascus (Z D P V 30:17). Danaba was, then, one of the four captured cities. But Shalmaneser's success was not decisive, and henceforth he had to

[1] Cf. Winckler, Das Vorgebirge am Nahr-el-Kelb, '09, p. 16.

give up the Syrian wars in favor of more urgent business in the far north.

At last Hazael was at liberty to wreak his vengeance on Israel. His first blows apparently fell upon Gilead and Bashan, which he "cut off" from Israel (2 Kings 10:32–33). Jehu may have appealed more than once to Shalmaneser. How terrible the revenge of Hazael was appears from Amos 1:3 — "They have threshed Gilead with iron threshing sledges." Hazael's action was a signal for all other neighbors to stretch out their hands for spoil, and so we find Philistines, Edomites, Ammonites, and even the Tyrians, "forgetting the bond of brotherhood" (Am. 1:9), making Razzias into Israel (Is. 9:12, Am. 1:6–15). Under Jehu's son Joahaz (814–797) Israel's abasement reached the extreme stage. Hazael's armies overran the entire land (G V J II 378). So ignominious were the conditions in these days that the records are silent of all details save the one fact that the Aramaeans only allowed Joahaz an army of 50 horsemen, 10 chariots and 10,000 men (more probably only 1000 men O L Z '01, 144, 2 Kings. 13:7).

Hazael's ambitions, it appears, were chiefly directed to the south, and he wisely abstained from giving offense to Assyria by undue efforts in the north. Arabia especially seems to have been close to his heart, for it was with the purpose of exercising more complete control over the Arabs that he pushed his conquests into Philistaea, where the Arabian caravan roads reached the sea.[1] Besides this the control of the coastal plain of Palestine gave him the monopoly of the trade with Egypt. According to the information of the Greek text of Lucian in 2 Kings 13:22, lost in the M.T., Hazael captured all of Philistaea as far as Aphek in Sharon. He even laid siege to Gath, and from there made an expedition against Jerusalem, whose king Joash paid him a rich tribute out of the temple treasury (2 Chr. 24:19 f., 2 Kings 12:18 f.). Thus Hazael looms up as a great warrior, the greatest, perhaps, of the Aramaean kings. He was on the best road to the realization

[1] It is possible that Hazael was of Arabian extraction, for we find a king of Aribi named Ḫazaîlu in the time of Essarhaddon; cf. Prisms A and C, III, 1 f.

of a Syrian-Arabian empire when death called him away from the throne.

Benhadad III assumed the reins of government at the very latest in 804 B.C. It would seem that Joahaz of Israel immediately seized the opportunity of a change of rulers at Damascus to shake off the foreign yoke.[1] According to a suggestion of Kuenen (Einleitung 25), the account of a seige of Samaria (2 Kings 6: 24–7:20) which, in its present connection, is placed in the time of Joram ben Ahab in reality seems to belong to the time of Joahaz. It is a priori unlikely that Joram should be meant, since Damascus was during his reign too occupied with the Assyrian danger to assume the offensive against Israel. The actual fighting that did occur at this time, furthermore, centered at Ramoth in Gilead (G V J II 362). That Joahaz alone can be meant becomes a certainty from 6: 32, where the king is called "son of a murderer," which must refer to Jehu, the father of Joahaz, whose bloody deeds are chronicled in detail (*l.c.* 379). The Benhadad of our story can well be the son of Hazael, for the prophet Elisha was alive still in the time of Joash the son of Joahaz. Benhadad, then, upon the denial of his suzerainty by Joahaz, marched against Israel and laid siege to Samaria. Dire need and starvation reigned soon in the city. The king's whole wrath was turned against Elisha, who could give no other counsel than "Trust in God." But the prophet's word was vindicated, for on the morrow the Aramaean war camp lay deserted. The cause of the flight of the enemy is sought in the approach of Hittite and Egyptian armies. Usually this is emended by historians into "Assyrian armies" and referred to the advance of Adadnirâri IV (810–782). Perhaps we should do better, however, to abide by the text and to understand *Miṣraim* as referring not to Egypt but to the northern "Muṣri", or Cappadocia. They and the Hittites of Carchemish and Arpad may well have been moved by the Haldians

[1] 2 Kings 13: 22 must then be regarded as inexact. Its late origin is recognized by commentators on other grounds than the one advanced here. Besides, Hazael died some time before 803, while Joahaz lived till 797.

of Urartu to attack Damascus, for the Haldians were striving to establish an empire in Syria about this time (cf. Ch. XII). The campaigns of Adadnirâri in 806 to Arpad, 805 to Ḫazāz, may have been directed against the Haldian power in this quarter. If our interpretation can be trusted, the siege of Samaria must have taken place about 806 B.C. Damascus, forced to fight the Haldians, had to release its pressure on Israel.

Certainly some events must have taken place which momentarily weakened Damascus. For Adadnirâri can boast on the stone-slab inscription that in one of his campaigns, probably that of 803 "to the sea," he laid siege to Damascus and received the tribute of its king Mari'.[1] This name is merely the popular title of the kings of Damascus, "my lord." The real name of the ruler can only have been Benhadad. Adadnirâri received from him in his palace 2300 talents of silver, 20 talents of gold, 3000 talents of copper, 5000 talents of iron, brightly colored garments, cloths, an ivory bed, a couch of inlaid ivory. In the same inscription he asserts that he made tributary to himself Hatti, Amurri, Tyre, Sidon, the land of Omri, Edom, and Philistaea. These glittering generalities, however, must be regarded with the greatest scepticism.

The renewed advance of the Assyrians gave Israel a breathing spell. Already in the reign of Joash (797–781) the Hebrews won successes against Aram. This is reflected in the oracle of the dying Elisha concerning "the Arrow of victory over Aram" (2 Kings 13: 14–19). From it we may at least gather that Joash administered a most severe defeat to Damascus at Aphek. The Assyrian campaign against Manṣuate in 797 may have helped to render the beginning of his reign auspicious, since Damascus was heavily engaged thereby. Joash succeeded in winning back the cities which his father had lost to Hazael. His successor

[1] As now appears from the Boghaz-Koī texts, the word Mar, "lord," is derived from the title "mariannu" borne by the Aryan nobility in Syria in the days of the Hittite empire. Adadnirâri is for some reason reverting back to this old title of city rulers in our instance, O L Z '10: 292 f.

Jeroboam II (781–740) even regained the Marsyas plain as far as the entrance to Hamath, and gave Israel a new period of bloom. The campaign of Shalmaneser IV (783–773) against Damascus in 773 and Ḫatarik in 772, mentioned in the Eponym chronicle, may have greatly aided Jeroboam. About this time the reign of Benhadad III must have drawn to its close. Valuable light is shed on the events in his last years by an Aramaic inscription from Hamath which we shall discuss in an especial chapter (Ch. XI).

CHAPTER X

KILAMMU OF SAM'AL

AMONG the north Syrian principalities we have already met that of Sam'al, at the foot of the Amanus mountains, and have heard of its King Ḫâni of Sam'al, alias Ḫaiâni son of Gabbar. The brilliantly successful excavations conducted by F. von Luschan on behalf of the German Oriental Society at Senğirli, have brought to light the capital and center of the kingdom of Sam'al and a number of valuable inscriptions of Sam'al's kings. The oldest of these inscriptions, found shattered to fragments, but completely restored by the skill of an expert of the Berlin Museum, is that of Kilammu son of Ḫaiâ.[1] Von Luschan straightway recognized that the Ḫaiâ mentioned can be no other than the Ḫâni of Sam'al who lived in the days of Shalmaneser.

The language of the inscription is Canaanitic or Phoenician. If it were not for the fact that its author calls himself "bar Ḫaiâ," using the Aramaic word "*bar*" for son, we would scarcely believe that he was an Aramaean, for there are hardly any traces of Aramaic in the rest of the inscription. Nevertheless the language of the invaders must have been spoken to a very large extent in this region at Kilammu's time and even earlier, for some geographical terms in the Assyrian inscriptions referring to this district are undoubtedly Aramaic; the name of the Kara-Su river as Saluara (El) river, is an example (S B A '92, 330). But the learned men of the land, the priests and scribes, were all of the older stock,

[1] A S 237 ff. makes no attempt to decipher the inscription. Its difficulties were, however, quickly solved by the work of Littmann, S B A '11: 976 f.; Lidzbarski, E S E III 218 f.; Bauer, Z D M G, 67: 684 f. Extremely divergent but not convincing is the interpretation of Hoffmann, Theol. Lit. Zeit., '12 (January 6).

and thus the Phoenician tongue, which had maintained itself in spite of centuries of Hittite domination, was used in the cult and in the civic administration.

The name of our king K L M V has been variously interpreted. Littmann vocalized it "Kalumu" (*l.c.* 978) and compared the personal name "Kalummu" (= "young") of the Hammurapi Dynasty. Streck (*ibid.* 985) calls attention to the Kulummai in M V A G '06, 230. But in view of such names as Giammu, Panammu, Tutammu, it seems preferable to regard that of this king as Hittite. The first element then is *Kil* — which is frequent in proper names of Asia Minor provenance;[1] the second element *mu* is then the ending — *moas*, — *mouas*, — *muēs*.[2] Lidzbarski suggests (*l.c.* 224) that the name Khēramuēs found on the island of Samos (Kretzschmer 333) is perhaps identical with "Kilammu."

Kilammu's inscription is divided into two portions by a double line drawn horizontally through the middle, and the material content of the inscription justifies this division. In the first half he deals with historical matter and in the second part with social and religious things. Let us follow his own story in detail.

After informing us who he is by the words "I am Kilammu son of Ḫaiâ," the author gives us a brief historical survey of his dynasty (2–5) and mentions as its founder a certain Gabbar whom we have heard of as the father of Ḫâni of Sam'al from Assyrian sources. As his name shows, Gabbar was an Aramaean. If he was contemporary of Ashurnazirpal, we see that already at this day the Aramaeans had seized the reins of government in Sam'al. This king's reign is described briefly as "Gabbar ruled over Ya'di[3] and accomplished nothing." Likewise his successor Bamah

[1] Cf. Lycian Kill-ortas, pisid. Kill-ares; also the place names Kilistra, Kilarazos (Kretzschmer, Einleitung in die Geschichte der Griechischen Sprache '96, p. 368). O L Z '11: 542 compares of Kili-Teshup (Hittite).

[2] Poiamoas, Oubramouasis, Panamues. Kretzschmer, *l.c.*, 332 f. As Lidzbarski points out, the final *vav* in KLMV must have had consonantal value for the *scriptio plena* for vowels does not occur in this inscription. This dispenses at once with all Semitic interpretations of the name.

[3] Ya'di = Sam'al; cf. Ch. XIV.

(B M H) accomplished nothing. The third king of the dynasty was the present ruler's father Ḫaiâ. Since he is called by the Assyrian "son of Gabbar," we must assume that Bamah was either an older brother of Ḫaiâ or else a usurper. Ḫaiâ, too, accomplished nothing. His name is given in the short hypocoristic form, while the Assyrian gives the fullest form Ḫaiâni. Perhaps the popular form was avoided in speaking to strangers; thus the bilingual texts from Palmyra give the hypocoristic form in the Aramaic portion, but the full form in the Greek (E S E III 225, II 282). The name Ḫaiân also appears in the later Nabataean inscriptions. It has been frequently pointed out that the name of the Hyksos king, Khian, recorded by Manetho, bears striking similarity to this Arabian-Aramaean Ḫaiân (S B A 11:979). Ḫaiâ was succeeded by Kilammu's brother She'īl [1] who "accomplished nothing." How Kilammu finally came to the throne is not said but it is quite likely that the murder of She'īl preceded his accession. Since Kilammu's name is unsemitic, he may have been the son of a Hittite wife of Ḫaiâ, and only a half-brother to Sheīl.

Peculiarly indeed Kilammu described himself as "son of perfection." It has been suggested that he is imitating the custom of Assyrian kings, who in praising themselves very often use the expression "*gitmalu,*" "perfect." [2] And Bauer (*l.c.* 685) has supposed that Kilammu̧ is playing on his name with the similar Assyrian "kalâmu" and calling himself "der Allesmacher" or the "one who accomplishes everything." For an Assyrian vassal it, of course, must have been eminently satisfactory that he was able to give his name such a flattering interpretation. And indeed this observation seems justified from the next sentence, in

[1] This would be the Aramaic vocalization. If it was spoken in Hebrew fashion, it would be Sha'ūl (= Saul). Littmann's interpretation "sha-ili," "of God," is less likely. Perhaps She'īl was Ḫaiâ's brother, not Kilammu's; E S E III 226 suggests that possibly the oldest member of the ruling family came to the throne as among the Osmanlis.

[2] Hehn, Bibl. Zeitschr., '12: 121. It seems unnecessary to hold with E S E III 227 that *bar Tam* is a proper name, "son of Tam," referring to the mother of Kilammu. It would be rather unusual for a Semite to mention his mother in this manner.

which this king shows a most remarkable self-esteem: "Of that which I accomplished the previous (kings) accomplished nothing." Thus the history of the dynasty culminates in himself, and before his glory the deeds of all other who sat on Sam'al's throne pale into insignificance.

Of his foreign policy he tells us in ll. 5–8, "My father's house," he says, "was in the midst of powerful kings." He does not name them, but we can imagine who most of them were. For Sam'al bordered to the north on Gurgum, to the south on Ḫattina, and Yaḫan, to the east on Bīt-Adini. And beyond these were numerous other kingdoms that were constantly forming new political constellations, and whose aid could be bought with gold. It was a perilous diplomatic game that was constantly being played at the royal courts of these petty states. "Every one (of these kings) stretched out his hand against (my people)" (Z D M G 68:227). Vividly in these few words our author paints the situation that existed in Syria since time immemorial. It was under such conditions that Kilammu came to the throne. And what was the result? Forcibly he relates: "But I became in the hands of the kings like a fire that devours beard and hand." [1] In this connection he gives us an incident: "When the king of the D — N Y M [2] arose against me, I hired against him the king of Ashur. A maiden he (the king of D.) had to give for every sheep, and a man for every garment." [3] Kilammu employs almost military terseness and brevity. The result of his adversary's hostility was disastrous to himself. The adversary had to pay him a large war indemnity.

Who is the king of D — N Y M? This problem is the most vexing one offered by our inscription. We are well acquainted

[1] Bauer, *l.c.*, 690. But the passage is interpreted also in various other ways. E S E III 228 translates, "I also was in the hand of kings, for devoured was my beard, devoured was my hand." Beard and hand typify a man's dignity and strength.

[2] Unfortunately the second letter of the name is illegible.

[3] Bauer, *l.c.*, 686 f. This interpretation is preferable to that of Lidzbarski, 231, who assumes that Kilammu made this payment to the king of Ashur.

with the various states of Syria from the Assyrian records, but there is no such name occurring among them. It would be tempting to correct the name into Y (Ḫ) N Y M — people of Yaḫan, but this is precarious. If we abide by the reading D — N Y M, it might be held that the Dodanim, a Greek tribe and branch of the Ionians, referred to in Genesis 10:4 are meant. In this case it must be assumed that sea-kings from Cyprus or other islands of the Mediterranean temporarily exercised power over the Amanus region. Then too it must be concluded that the Assyrian king on an oversea's venture subjected this Greek king and forced him to pay an indemnity. While this is not impossible *per se*, we must be rather skeptical in regard to such an expedition. Another possibility is that advocated by Littmann, that the tribe or people of Danuna is here referred to, which appears among the Asiatics in the Egyptian annals (M A E 359) and occurs in a letter of Abimilki king of Tyre (Kn. no. 151:52). The locality referred to is disputed. The only indication we have is the fact that it is mentioned along with Ugarit. The latter seems to have been a seaport in the extreme north of Syria (Kn. 1017). In one of the Boghaz-Koï tablets the Hittite king justifies himself before the king of Babylon because a caravan bound for Amurru and Ugarit was attacked within his territory (M D O G no. 35, p. 24). In our Amarna letter the Hittite army is also mentioned. It is therefore undeniably plausible that a small state or people of Danuna may have existed in the ninth century in the vicinity of Alexandrette on the western slopes of the Amanus. This people was fairly safe from attack by the Assyrians, and need therefore not be mentioned in the inscriptions of the latter. On the other hand it might through the pass of Beilân encroach upon the territory of Sam'al or at least make razzias into this region.[1] An additional explanation which has not yet been proffered might be this, that the country of Daiaeni on the Upper Euphrates is referred to by D — N Y M. A temporary expansion of power from

[1] The city of Dinanu given in the list R T P 15 and lying in the vicinity of Aleppo might also claim consideration.

this center south to the region of Sam'al is not impossible. Still better, however, might be the supposition that (Bît)-Zamâni is meant,[1] a state in the Kashiar region against which the Assyrians in these days made a number of campaigns (cf. Toffteen, Researches, p. 6ff.).

Whoever the hostile king was, Kilammu "hired against him the king of Ashur" (cp. 2 Sam. 10:6). We do not hear what measures the Assyrian took, nor have we any clue in the cuneiform inscriptions. The Assyrian help, however, was effective. Kilammu retained his independence, and the large indemnity which he received, coupled with the care-free life that he could now live under Assyria's protection, enabled him to devote his attention to the promotion of the common weal.

About such peaceful endeavors, Kilammu tells us in the second part of his inscription. Herein lies his greatest pride. Like Solomon of Israel, he was a diplomat, a builder, an organizer, rather than a warrior. But his idea of the relation of a king to his subjects is singularly different from that recorded of Solomon and other Oriental potentates. What the word "Landesvater" expresses to the German appears to have been the ideal of Kilammu.

The second part begins anew with an introduction in which the king names himself. We find the same form in the Assyrian annals, as well as in the Phoenician monuments (cf. Eshmunazzar, 13). "I Kilammu, son of Ḫaiâ, sat on the throne of my father. Before the previous kings the inhabitants walked (i.e. were considered) like dogs."[2] Forcefully, though not unjustly the author describes the character of the Oriental despots. But how different was his own way! "I on the contrary was a father to the one, a mother to the next, a brother to the third" (cf. Bauer *l.c.* 688). He also brought prosperity to the poor and miserable. "Him, who never saw the face of a sheep, I made the possessor of

[1] The change of Z into D is no obstacle, as that is frequent; cf. Ḫindān and Ḫinzān, Z A 19: 236.

[2] Cf. E S E III 233. Another interpretation, "slunk about like dogs," is offered, Z D M G 68: 227.

a flock and him who never saw the face of an ox, I made the possessor of cattle, and owner of silver and owner of gold, and him who from his youth had never seen cotton, I covered in my day with byssus." What a contrast to the poverty and utter neglect of human needs in former times! No wonder that as he thinks back and recalls former conditions he comes to the judgment that his predecessors accomplished nothing! "But I stood as support at the side of the inhabitants, and they showed me a feeling such as the feeling of an orphan for a mother." Thus the ideal state, Kilammu believes, was achieved under his rule.

Like all those who erect monuments for posterity, Kilammu fears nothing so much as that his memory might be forgotten. Therefore he adjures the coming generations: "If any one of my descendants who shall sit in my stead, shall bring libation to this inscription, (under him) the Mushkab shall not oppress the Ba'rîr and the Ba'rîr shall not oppress the Mushkab." [1] He thus invokes a blessing upon the reign of his successor who honors his monument. And the greatest benefit that he can think of for a King of Sam'al is peace between two factions that were powerful in this state. It has been suggested that Mushkab represents the inhabitants or fellahin, while Ba'rîr designates the Beduin. Still more likely, however, is the view (E S E III 235) that the difference is more a national than a cultural one, and that the Mushkab is the old inhabitant of Canaanite or Hittite stock, while the Ba'rîr is the Aramaean immigrant who now formed an important part of the population. This indeed strikes the truth squarely, for the word Ba'rîr is used in the later Aramaic in the sense of barbarian or foreigner. Since the two words appear without the article they are semi-proper names. The Aramaeans therefore continued to be called Ba'rîr long after they

[1] The word "Mushkab" must refer to human beings, as proceeds from the contrast to Ba'rîr in l. 14. The translation "sepulchers" is impossible. E S E III 233 correctly suggests that it means inhabitants of a lower order. The Babylonia "Mushkênu," so frequent in the Hammurapi code, might be regarded as analogous. Bauer, *l.c.*, 687, explains the expression "Mushkab" as "dwelling" used for "dwellers," just as Assyrian bît often means "tribe."

had ceased to be nomads and had taken up agriculture and trade. The linguistic and racial differences between the two factions made a sharp distinction necessary in the affairs of the kingdom and increased the difficulties of the sovereign. The modus vivendi presupposed by Kilammu is exactly like that in early Shechem between Hebrew and Canaanite. But the possibility of bloody strife arising at any moment, as happened in Shechem, seems dreadful to him.

The rite which Kilammu hopes shall be evermore performed at his monument, the libation,[1] has its analogy in Semitic usage. Thus Sennacherib (Prism VI 66f.) says that whoever of his descendants that shall reign after him shall have to renovate his palace, "May he gaze upon the inscription of my name, may he anoint it with oil, bring sacrifice, and return it to its place; then Ashur and Ishtar shall hear his prayer." To anoint an inscription of one's forebears with oil was thus an act of respect and veneration, incumbent upon those who were pious. But as Sennacherib closes his inscription with a curse upon the head of him who shall change the writing of his name, so Kilammu also concludes "whoever shall destroy this inscription, may Ba'al Ṣemed who is Gabbar's (god) destroy his head, and Ba'al Ḫaman, who is Bamah's (god), destroy his head, and Rekabel, Ba'al of my house."

In this oath formula lies the only indication that we have of Kilammu's religious life. He mentions three royal patrons that have proved themselves helpful to the kings of Sam'al. Nor can it be accidental that above his inscription there are engraved three divine symbols. The first of these symbols, to the left, is the horned head-dress usually worn by the gods in ancient sculptures; the second is undoubtedly the bridle of a horse;[2] the third is the waning moon with a superimposed full moon. The god Ba'al Ṣemed, "lord of the team" (of oxen), is an agri-

[1] So Bauer, *l.c.*, 689. Lidzbarski and others translate "damage," which is unlikely. The remainder of the quotation has likewise been correctly explained by Bauer, *ibid.*

[2] So Hehn convincingly proves, Biblische Zeitschrift, 1912, p. 116.

cultural deity and may be meant with the first symbol. To define Ba'al Ḫaman is more difficult. The interpretation "Lord of the Amanus" is untenable (E S E III 236). The name must be derived from the Canaanite *ḫamōn*, which primarily signifies "noise, roar, tumult." We should therefore regard this divinity as a storm-god, and the equivalent of Hadad; and since Hadad is a variation of the moon god in his rôle of weathermaker (G G 88), the third symbol can represent Ba'al-Ḫamōn. Hommel's supposition (G G 160) that the Carthaginian Ba'al Ḫaman represents the waning moon is thus vindicated. Rekabel "The charioteer (or rider) is god" is the old Aramaean war-god and is a manifestation of the God Amar (O L Z '09:16). His symbol must thus be the bridle. But though Kilammu recognizes these gods and calls upon them to curse impiety, he does not give any credit to them for past help. As long as he lives he does not need them; when he is dead they may guard his inscription! How differently does a Panammu speak of the grace of the Gods! Lack of the reverence which he demands of others is characteristic of Kilammu. He has neither respect for his ancestors nor for the divine powers. He is Kilammu, "son of perfection."

His relation to Assyria is not clear. The expression "I hired the king of Assyria" is noticeably contemptuous. He is ungrateful, however, for without Assyrian help his prosperity would have been impossible. But we must ask ourselves — was he still a subject of Assyria at the time of this inscription and would a vassal have dared to speak in this fashion? It is quite possible that he wrote this inscription at the time of Shalmaneser IV (783–773), when Assyria was greatly weakened. But on the other hand it is singular that Kilammu has no weapon, but peacefully holds in his hand a flower,[1] while in pre-Assyrian sculptures from Senğirli weapons are always represented. (E S E III 230.) This seems to indicate that Kilammu is still a vassal, and that it was

[1] Is the flower a symbol of the moongod? According to Hommel, G G 88, Nannar is pictured as "lily." Nannar-In-shushinak, God of Shushan, the city of the "lily," III R 55 No. 3, 24 bc.

forbidden to vassals to wear weapons or to allow themselves to be portrayed with them. Assyria's prestige, however, is so small, and Kilammu's notion of his own greatness so exaggerated, that it is only a little step to a declaration of independence.

Kilammu, we must conclude, was a wise and able ruler. If we set aside his impiety and conceit, we have a man of sagacious and kindly character. His inscription, however, was destroyed despite the curses, which the foe who sacked the city may not have understood. Thousands of years later, however, the skill of the modern scientist has restored the fragments to a living whole.

CHAPTER XI

ZAKIR OF HAMATH AND LA'ASH

As we have already indicated, Hamath's rise to power is synchronous with the decay of Ḫattina. The capital city, called also Hamath Rabbah,[1] or the "great Hamath" (Am. 6:2), is identical with the modern Ḥamā on the Orontes and the classical Epiphania. The great Tell in the middle of the present city contains the remains of this ancient capital of the second largest state of Syria, and an excavation of it should yield rich treasures in inscriptions and monuments. The location of Ḥamā has always been one of commercial importance, situated as it is on the great highway from the Biqâ' and Damascus to Aleppo and in the vicinity of one of the most fruitful districts of central Syria. If the interpretation of its name as meaning "Metropolis" (König) be correct, as seems likely, then its commercial and political character is sufficiently emphasized. It was doubtless an ancient Canaanitic settlement (cf. Gen. 10:18) and then became a center of Hittite influence, as is affirmed by the discovery there of the so-called "Hamath stones," or Hittite inscriptions.[2] Its king Irḫuleni, who fought at Qarqar, was a last scion of the Hittite nobility in this part of Syria. But the population of his country must have been largely Aramaean.

The northern border of Hamath in Shalmaneser's day must have been near Idlib, southwest of Aleppo, where we found the frontier towns of Adennu, Bargâ and Arganâ. Later it reached as far north as il-Athārib, as will appear shortly. Two excellent strongholds guarded Hamath, which itself is undefended, on the

[1] A reminiscence of Rabbah may be seen in Qal'at er-Rubbeh a little west of Ḥamā.

[2] Cf. Garstang, The Land of the Hittites, 93 f.

north — Apamea and Larissa. In its best days Hamath controlled the entire Bargylus region together with a number of important coast cities like Usnu, Siannu Ṣimirra, Rashpuna.[1] Its southern border must be defined, by the familiar Old Testament expression Lābō Hamath, "the entrance to Hamath," with which Israel's ideal northern frontier is described. This can only designate that point where the Orontes river leaves the Biqâ' and flows into the valley between Lebanon and Antilebanon. Near this point there is a town to-day called Lebweh and in ancient times Libum; it is very likely, as is supposed by some, that the verbal form Lābō hās crystallized into the mane of this place in later days. And if we read in Numbers 34:11 that Harbelah (LXX while M T has Riblah) is Israel's border we find this preserved in the modern il Harmel north of Libum (Z A W 3:274). But apart from this indirect argument, we know definitely that the territory of Hamath extended at least to Riblah, south of the lake of Ḥoms (cf. 2 Kings 23: 33 etc.).

Hamath, after the death of Benhadad II of Damascus, seems to have given up resistance against Assyria, in order to avoid further demolition of its cities. Indeed, it became a supporter of Assyria, for the attack of Adadnirâri IV against Mari' of Damascus, as well as of Shalmaneser against Hazael, is unthinkable except under the supposition that the Assyrians allowed Hamath to annex some of the territory of Ḫattina, when that state was reduced to Unqi–il 'Amq. It was good policy for them to strengthen Hamath at the expense of other less loyal states. However, it was only natural that, as soon as Assyria failed to assert its power in the west, the other states of Syria should seek to avenge themselves upon Hamath for its Assyrian partisanship.

These conditions are reflected in a most remarkable inscription, discovered and edited by Pognon.[2] It is written in a dialect that is Aramaic in many characteristics, but in which a Canaanitic

[1] We shall deal with the so-called "19 districts of Hamath" in Chapter XII.

[2] Inscriptions sémitiques de la Syrie, de la Mésopotamie et de la région de Mossoul, 1907, No. 86.

vocabulary predominates (J B L 28:64). It takes us, therefore, to the period of the Aramaean absorption of this region, and throws an unexpected flood of light on the history of Hamath in the obscure period between Shalmaneser and Tiglathpileser. The inscription unfortunately is not fully preserved. It was once written upon a monolith of at least 2:10 meters height (according to the discoverer's estimate), which no doubt the Arabs broke into blocks for building purposes. Four of these blocks were recovered and the largest exhibits the relief of the lower extremities of a human figure.

Whom this sculpture once represented is related in the opening line of the inscription: "The stele which Zakir,"[1] king of Hamath and La'ash placed for Elūr (and inscribed"). This title of the inscription straightway raises the question, what is meant by La'ash. A city or region so important that it can be named alongside of Hamath should be mentioned in the Assyrian inscriptions, or in the Old Testament. But the cuneiform records seem to leave us in the lurch entirely. In Genesis 10:19, however, we may have an occurrence of it if the conjecture that Lasha' is an error for La'ash be true (Procksch 79). There the border of the Canaanite habitat is described as running from Sidon to Gerar (near Gaza), then east to Sodom, and then north again to Lasha'. We are led to expect that Lasha' lies somewhere east of Phoenicia, in order to complete the quadrangle. Montgomery has discovered references in the early Arabic Geographies to a town of Bal'âs[2] in the region of Ḥoms (J B L 28:69) which is to-day preserved in the Ğebel Bil'âs southeast of Selemiyeh (E S E III 176). If this be the neighborhood of the ancient La'ash, then its omission in the cuneiform inscriptions is explicable by the analogy of the near-by

[1] This vocalization given by Pognon is retained by us here because of the occurrence of this form among the Mesopotamian names. Nöldeke (Z A XXI 375 ff.) reads Zakur and Montgomery, Zakar. Kn. 1095 compares the prince Zikar from the same region in Amarna days.

[2] Montgomery, *l.c.*, 70, also reminds us of the startling similarity between the names La'ash and Lagash in Babylonia, and finds a Balâs between Waṣīt and Basra.

Tadmor (Palmyra), which is also never mentioned, since it lies too far to the left of the highway. But, on the other hand, Bil'âs lies far north of the latitude of Sidon, which seems rather a serious objection. For the present the view of Dussaud appears preferable. He identifies La'ash with Luḫuti (R A '08, 222 f.). This is philologically plausible and historically most highly probable. As we have seen (Ch. VIII) the land of Luḫuti is the lofty Bargylus plateau, which seems to have belonged to Hamath in the days of Ashurnazirpal. It represents a conquered province of Hamath rather than an integral original part of the kingdom. What is more likely than that a ruler of Hamath should include Luḫuti in his title, and call himself "King of Hamath and Luḫuti"? It is certainly more probable than that the obscure Bil'âs should appear in the title.[1] This would only be possible if it be the birthplace of Zakir or the first city of his rule.

After designating the stele as dedicated to the god Elûr, the author begins anew "Zakir, King of Hamath and La'ash, a humble man am I" (1–2).[2] And because of his great humility he received divine aid: "And (there helped me) Ba'alshamayn and stood by me and Ba'alshamayn made me king over Hazrak" (3–4). It would appear that Zakir was the organizer of a rebellion in this city, and became its king and that from here he subdued the rest of the kingdom. What the political cause of his rebellion was is not quite clear, but we may assume that in all probability the king of Hamath had yielded to the pressure of his neighbors, especially of Damascus, to join an anti-Assyrian coalition, and that the pro-Assyrian party had raised Zakir to the throne in one of the chief strongholds of the realm. It is but natural that the southern part of the kingdom near the border of Damascus should be hostile to this dangerous neighbor.

The fortress of Hazrak is identical with the Hadrach of Zechariah 9:1—"Jahve is in the land of Hadrach and in Damascus is his seat."

[1] As historically, if not philologically, unlikely I also regard the view of Grimme, O L Z '09:15, that La'ash = Alashia (Cyprus).

[2] E S E III 6 suggests "man from 'Anā" (or Akko?). I prefer "humble," and find here a striking analogy to the Messianic predicate Zech. 9: 9.

It occurs in the cuneiform inscriptions as Ḫatarikka. The name is considered to be of Hittite origin by Lidzbarski who thinks that the initial Ḫ in Ḫamath, Ḫalman, Ḫadrach may be a word meaning fortress or city (E S E III 175).[1] There can be no doubt but that the Zakir inscription originally stood in the city of Hadrach. Pognon conceals all information as to the place of discovery of the stele, but as Lidzbarski has seen, it doubtless was found at Umm-esh-Shershûḫ situated on a high long Tell above the Orontes northwest of Tell Bisê and south of ir-Restân, the classical Arethusa (E S E III 174 f.). It holds a commanding position on the important highway to the Biqâ'. Here Lidzbarski found in the wall of a house part of a relief of Assyro-Aramaean character, showing the upper part of a man's body, the hand uplifted in gesture of adoration, hair and beard curled, and wearing a tiara with feathers and a horn curved upward above the brow (E S E III 167 f.). The missing part of the Zakir stele must have been quite similar. Here then lay ancient Hadrach, the importance of which disappeared with the rise of Ḥoms, as had that of Kadesh with the rise of Hadrach.

Our inscription now relates how the great coalition immediately attempted to suppress the rebellion and to capture Hazrak. "And Barhadad, son of Hazael, king of Aram, united against me (seven)-teen kings" (4–5). We thus have an astonishing and important reference to Benhadad III of Damascus. There now follows a list of kings, which, however, cannot have included 17 names. Seven are preserved: "Barhadad and his war-camp, Bargush[2] and his camp, the king of Que and his camp, the king of 'Amq and his camp, the king of Gurgum and his camp, the king of Sam'al and his camp, and the king of Miliz[3] (and his

[1] It is tempting to find in Hadrach the name of the moongod Aku. If it were not for the form Ḫazrak, we should translate it "sacred enclosure of Aku."

[2] As Schiffer first saw (S A IV), Bargush is the "apil Gusi" occurring often in the Assyrian inscriptions as a term for the king of Arpad. Gush is perhaps a divine name; it occurs also in "N R G S H." C I S II 105; cf. E S E III 7.

[3] Miliz was correctly identified by Dussaud with the Armenian Milid (Malatia).

camp)" . . . (5–7). In the lacuna of line 8 there is room for possibly three more names; then at the end of line 8 and in line 9 we must read with Pognon "seven kings they and their camps." These seven unspecified kings, with the three missing and the seven given names make up the number seventeen.[1]

Vividly Zakir proceeds to give details of the siege of Ḫazrak. "And all these kings laid siege against Ḫazrak, and raised a wall higher than the wall of Ḫazrak, and dug a ditch, deeper than the ditch of Ḫazrak" (G–19). The procedure is very similar to that described in the siege of Abel Beth Ma'acah (2 Sam. 20:15 f.). The purpose of these engineering operations was to undermine the wall of the city so that it should fall at some point and make a breach for the attackers. The allies, however, were unsuccessful. Piously Zakir assigns his deliverance to his patron Ba'alshamayn: "I lifted up my hands unto Ba'alshamayn, and Ba'alshamayn answered me and Baalshamayn said unto me through the instrumentality of seers and the instrumentality of counters" (11–12). The word of the gods, therefore, came to the king through the mouth of diviners. The "seers" are familiar to us from the Old Testament, but the "counters" form a new class. They are probably astrologers. As has been suggested, the word has its parallel in the Babylonian "dupshar minâti" or "writer of numbers" a class of diviners.[2] In this manner then "Baalshamayn (said), 'Fear not, for I made thee king and I will stand by thee and I will deliver thee from all (the kings which) have laid against thee a siege'" (13–15). Unfortunately our account here becomes extremely fragmentary. Pognon estimates that with the loss of the upper part of the stele some thirty lines of the inscription which is continued on the narrow face of the left-hand side, are missing. They must have reported the events leading up to the raising of the siege. Evidently there was mention of the clash

[1] Cf. Montgomery, *l.c.*, 60.

[2] J B L 28: 69. Montgomery also suggests in that connection that the father of the prophet Azariah (2 Chron. 15: 1) and another prophet named Oded (2 Chron, 28: 9) never bore such a name, but that this was really the official title "counter, diviner."

of battle, for chariots and horsemen are spoken of and a king is described as in the midst of the fray (block III 2–3). The upshot of it all was the victory of Zakir and the discomfiture of the hostile coalition.

Peculiar circumstances, similar perhaps to those of 2 Kings 7:6, must have made the deliverance of Zakir possible. We have pointed out that his rebellion must have been due to the Anti-Assyrian policy of the king of Hamath, which finds its explanation in the weakness of Assyria and the peril from powerful neighbors. If so, then it is most likely that Assyrian aid caused Zakir's triumph over the hostile coalition, and helped him to gain Hamath and La'ash. Do the cuneiform records lend us any clues?

The suggestion has been made that the campaign of Adadnirâri IV in 803 against Mari' had some connection with Zakir's relief (J B L 28:62). But this seems to me unlikely. Our inscription mentions among the foes of Zakir the king of 'Amq. The last trace of the kingdom of Ḫattina dated from 832. Its reduction to the 'Amq must have taken place because of hostility toward Assyria. During the reign of Shalmaneser, about which we are quite fully informed, this cannot have come about, much less in the time of Shamshi-Adad (825–813), who did not concern himself with the west-land. But it is most plausible that Ḫattina should have been forced by Vannic influence (ch. XII) to resist Adadnirâri, as did its neighbor Arpad in 806; the campaign against Ḫazāz, the Ḫattina city, in 805 raises this to a certainty. And since the campaign against Damascus in 803 presupposes at least the passive aid of Hamath, I regard it as most likely that Hamath was rewarded by districts cut off from Ḫattina, which since then was called 'Amq. We must therefore seek a slightly later date for our events.

For the year 773 the Eponym list records a campaign of Shalmaneser against Damascus. This *eo ipso* indicates that Damascus was the heart of an anti-Assyrian coalition which did not include Hamath, since the expedition must have been undertaken from Hamath as a base. In the following year Shalmaneser died.

This gave the vigilant Benhadad and his allies a new opportunity of preparing against Assyria, and the Vannic state in the north gladly aided him. A coalition of seventeen states is formed, among them such northern principalities as Que, Gurgum, Sam'al and Melid, which were tributaries of Urartu. The one state loyal to Assyria, Hamath, was thus greatly imperiled and so its king chose to abandon his allegiance to Ashur and to join the allies. The pro-Assyrian party in Hamath, however, organized a rebellion and raised Zakir to the throne in the stronghold of Hadrach. The allied forces attempted to suppress this rebellion, but were defeated by the appearance of an Assyrian relief expedition. This expedition was one of the first acts of the new Assyrian king Ashurdan, for the Eponym list mentions as the salient fact of the year 772 "to the land of Hatarikka" (Hadrach). It may be that in the battle before the gates of this city Benhadad III lost his life and that Ṭāb'el (Is. 7:6) now became ruler of Damascus. What the purpose of the later campaigns against Hatarikka in 765 and 755 under Ashurdan and his successor may have been we do not know. It is possible that they had some connection with the pressure of Israel against the southern border of Hamath under the brilliant rule of Jeroboam II (cf. 2 Kings 14:25, 28).

The lines 4–15 of the third block of the Zakir inscription deal with the building operations of our ruler. "I (enlarged) Hadrach," he tells us, "and ad(ded to it) the whole surrounding district . . . . and filled it with . . . (and built) these fortifications on every side. I built houses for the gods in my whole land and built . . . and the cistern(?) . . . the temple (of Elûr) and I erected before (Elûr) this stele and wro(te up)on it the inscription of my hands." His main efforts, in great contrast to Kilammu of Sam'al, were devoted to strengthening the defenses of his realm and of building temples for the gods that had helped him.

The inscription closes with the customary imprecations 11:16–28—"Whoever causes the inscrip(tion of the hands) of Zakir, king of Hamath and La'ash to disappear from this monument or whoever causes this monument to disappear from before

Elûr or robs it away from its place, or whoever sends forth against it (his hand) . . . may Ba'alshamayn and E(lûr) . . . and Shamash and Shahr and . . . and the Gods of the heavens and the gods of the earth and Ba'al of La' (Ash) his roots (extirpate)."...

Zakir's inscription was erected "befor Elûr."[1] We may consequently assume that Elûr had a sanctuary in Hadrach at which the monument once stood. And the phraseology makes it likely that the inscription was composed by a Canaanite priest (E S E III 3). But who is the god Elûr?[2] It seems that Elûr is none other than the god Amar,[3] so frequently mentioned in the Assyrian inscriptions as god of the west-land. (O L Z '09, 16.) And what should be more likely than that on the edge of Amurrû, and on the great highway that leads through Amurrû, this divinity should be worshiped? He is probably the moon-god, not the solar deity (against Clay p. 108) for i-lu-mi-ir (= Elûr) appears among the names of Adad. C T 29:45 ll. 18–24 (O L Z 13:254.) But most peculiar is the fact that Zakir, although he erects the Stele to Elûr, gives glory only to Ba'alshamayn "lord of the heavens." It would be most tempting to assume that Ba'alshamayn is only an epithet or else a manifestation of Elûr. It should be noted that the great list of the gods (C T XXIV 40, 48) equates the god of the west-land (M A R — T U) with the "Adad of the deluge." Adad is merely a manifestation of the moon as the weather-maker. And to Adad the invocation of Ḫattusil in the treaty with Rameses applies the epithet Ba'alshamayn, as well as to his variant Reshef and to the Sun-god (M V A G '02, 5, 17, and M A E 311). Among the Hittites Adad or his synonym appears as the head of the pantheon

[1] O L Z '08:341 would read El-wadd. Wadd is an epithet for the moon-god of the Minaeans (G G 86). But *d* and *r* are carefully distinguished (J B L 28:66).

[2] The name of the antediluvian king Aloros mentioned by Berossus, as well as the town of Alouros in Judaea remind one very much of El-ur; cf. E S E III 5 and Clay, p. 158.

[3] If Schiffer's interpretation (O L Z '09:478) of Babylonian Expedition of the U. of P., Vol. X, no. 125, be right, the name KUR. GAL (= Amurru)-upaḫḫir is transcribed in the Aramaic "indorsement" as Ur-upaḫḫir, thus establishing the identity of Amar and Ūr.

and as god of the heavens (G G 51), so that the Hittite origin of Ba'alshamayn is very plausible (E S E II 250 f). It should be recalled also that Adōdos is called King of the Gods by Philo of Byblus (Frag. Gr. Hist. III 509). Shams and Shahr are the Arabian forms of the sun and moon gods. The conjectural Ba'al of La('ash) in l.26 (J B L 28:61) is a Phoenician local deity.

CHAPTER XII

NORTHERN SYRIA UNDER THE VANNIC KINGS

LIKE a great rampart of crescent shape, a series of mountain ranges frowns upon Assyria and Babylonia from the north. In the heart of these ranges lurked the hour of doom for every civilization that has arisen in the valley of the Euphrates and Tigris. From Iran or from the Caucasus or from the Taurus the great non-Semitic migrations poured into Semitic lands. Since the earliest days, therefore, we find the Assyro-Babylonian kings carrying war into these rugged regions for the purpose of sheer self-preservation.

At the headwaters of the river Tigris, there appears in the ninth century, B.C., an organized state of Urartu under a king named Arame.[1] Shalmaneser regarded it as so menacing to Assyria's interest that he undertook an expedition thither in 857, destroyed the capital Arzashkun, penetrated as far as lake Van, and left his inscription on Mount Irritia. The upstart state had been crushed no sooner than established. Some years later, however, we find that a reorganization has taken place in this region and that a new dynasty of kings founded by Sarduris I is flourishing there. These monarchs, who have left us numerous inscriptions, style themselves "Kings of Biaina (Van) ruling in Tuspa." The real name of the people they represent is "Haldians." Their rise is swift and glorious. Hardy sons and a rugged climate, possessing impenetrable retreats, they could swoop down like eagles from their fastnesses upon the Syrian and Mesopotamian towns.

The far-seeing Shalmaneser grasped fully the rôle the Vannic

[1] As his name indicates, this king was of Aramaean stock, perhaps a bold chieftain from the Tūr 'Abdīn who succeeded in establishing a state among the Alarodian northerners.

kings were destined to play in history. Two paths nature had marked out for them. The one led down the Tigris into Mesopotamia and Assyria, and threatened the very existence of the latter state. The other led down the Euphrates into northern Syria and to the sea, and menaced Assyria's position as a world power. And already in these early days the Vannic state made its power felt along the plane of its destiny. For this reason we find that Shalmaneser, immediately after crushing Bīt-Adini, turned his attention to Urartu. And after the campaign against Damascus in 846 he straightway in the following year marched to the Subnat grotto and there left an inscription commemorating the defeat of Benhadad and Irḫuleni and their allies. This is only comprehensible if the Haldians were, to say the least, silent partners in the Syrian league. We may therefore surmise (with Lehman-Haupt: Israel, 75) that the various campaigns to Que and other northern states from 840–829 and even the internal troubles in Que (834) and in Kinalua (832) have some relation to Haldian intrigues. Shamshi-Adad (825–813) also undertook campaigns against Ispuinis of Urartu, under whose rule many inscriptions in the native tongue of the Haldians were erected in Armenia. Ispuinis and his son Menuas, who for a time was coregent with his father, erected a bilingual inscription in the Kelishin pass on the boundary between Assyria and Urartu.

Under Adadnirâri IV the Haldian influence in northern Syria, which as we have pointed out, was largely responsible for the resistance of Arpad and Hattina in 806 and 805, and which strengthened the league headed by Benhadad III, was temporarily stemmed. In brilliant campaigns the Assyrian king seems to have subjected all Syria and Palestine. His alliance with Babylonia through the marriage with the famous Semiramis greatly increased the strength of his position. His successor, Shalmaneser IV, however, had to undertake six campaigns against Argistis I of Urartu, who once advanced within a few days' journey of Nineveh itself. Assyria was now entirely on the defensive. All the actions in Syria (773) against Damascus, (772, 765, 755) against

Hadrach must probably be viewed as directed against Urartu. Argistis I thus appears as a great conqueror, who expanded his realm far into Asia Minor and Syria, and who has left us his annals inscribed on the rocks of the citadel of Van. And it might indeed have fared worse with Assyria, had not a brave and brilliant war chief, Shamash-ilu, who served under three kings, been captain of the Assyrian hosts. (Lehman Haupt 82.)

Any advance of the Haldians down the Euphrates and into Syria brought them straight to the gates of Arpad. This state was therefore in a difficult position; it was forced to choose between Urartu and Assyria, and that choice was liable to have disastrous consequences. Urartu quite naturally exerted every means of "moral suasion" to have the help of Arpad, since Arpad was an excellent buffer against Assyria, behind which the Haldians could safely do what they pleased in Syria. And Arpad seems to have allowed itself to be persuaded. Even after the lesson administered to it by Adadnirâri IV in 806, it showed itself repeatedly antagonistic to the Assyrians. For the year 754 the eponym list mentions a campaign of Ashurnirâri to Arpad. This bald statement of the chronicle is illumined by a unique document that has come down to us — a treaty between king Mati-ilu of Arpad and Ashurnirâri (M V A G '98:228). The former surrendered to the Assyrian, and was allowed to retain his throne, but under most humiliating conditions. The treaty is sealed by the sacrifice of a goat. It tells:

> If Mati-lui sins against the oaths
> Then, just as this goat is brought up from his herd
> So that he will not return to his herd (will not
> again take his place at the head of his herd,)
> So shall Mati-ilu with his sons, his daughters,
> The people of his country (be brought up) from his land,
> To his land he shall not return at the head of his
> land (he shall not again take his place)
> This head is not the head of the goat
> It is the head of Mati-ilu.

(It is) the head of his children, his nobles, the
people of his country.
If Mati-ilu (transgress) against these oaths
Just as the head of the goat is cut off
— his teeth layed in his mouth —
So shall the head of Mati-ilu be cut off."

After this ritual ceremony, the conditions of Mati-ilu's vassalship are described as follows:

"At the command of Ashurnirâri he will go against
his (the Assyrian's) enemies.
Mati-ilu with his nobles, his forces,
According to their own pleasure they will not go
forth, not depart,
(else) Sin the great lord who dwells in Harran shall
clothe Mati-ilu
his nobles, the people of his country with leprosy
like a garment
that they must camp outside, without receiving mercy . . .
If Mati-ilu, his sons, his nobles or any one else
sins against
the oaths of Ashurnirâri, king of Assyria,
then his peasants shall not sing a harvest song
nor shall a plant of the field spring up."

Other more ignominious and debasing curses are also included, and at the close, a list of gods is invoked as witnesses, among them the Adad of Kurbân and the Adad of Ḫallaba.

During the lifetime of Ashurnirâri Mati-ilu seems to have kept his pledges. But the accession of a new king, Tiglathpileser IV (745–728), must have tempted him to rebel. The Eponym list mentions for the year 743 "in the city of Arpad;[1] the army of

[1] Does this mean that he entered the city? If so, then the view of Belck and Lehmann, p. 324 f., and Maspero, III 146, that Arpad opened its gates to him and served as a base of operations, would be correct.

Urartu defeated." Urartu and Arpad are here expressly joined together. The king of Urartu was the vigorous Sarduris II, who had made successful inroads into Assyria's northern possessions, and was now undertaking an invasion of Syria. His ambitions in this direction are manifested by the title which he adds to his name — "King of Suri." He had succeeded in forming a strong coalition against Assyria, including Mati-ilu of Arpad, Sumalal of Melid, Tarḫulara of Gurgum and Kundashpi of Kummuḫ (Ann. 596). Tiglathpileser seems to have advanced first against Arpad and to have left a strong force there to hold Mati-ilu in check. Thereupon he marched north and met the remainder of the alliance in battle between Kishtan and Ḫalpi in the land of Kammuḫ, winning a decisive victory. Sarduris, to save his life, had to flee on the back of a mare — a disgrace for any warrior.[1]

In the following year Tiglathpileser began the siege of Arpad in earnest. But the city did not fall until 740. Mati-ilu could expect no mercy from the Assyrians, and therefore chose to hold out to the bitter end. Without doubt he still hoped for help from Sarduris, but if so the hope was vain. Concerning the siege of the fortress we know nothing. That it was grimly defended the length of the siege reveals. Heartrending scenes of misery and starvation must have occurred within those doomed walls. Its final capture must have been followed by a gruesome vengeance upon Mati-ilu and his people. On that day the curses of Ashurnirâri came true. Even for another century the city remained a terrible example of Assyrian revenge (cf. 2 Kings 18:34, Is. 10:9, Jer. 49:23). And so deep was the impression upon the Syrian states of that day that the various princes paid Tiglathpileser tribute and thus temporarily renounced their allegiance to Urartu. Among them were Raṣun (Rezin) of Damascus, and the kings of Kummuḫ, Que, Tyre, Carchemish, and Gurgum.

Only one did not appear with tribute of whom it was expected — Tutammu of Unqi. He evidently contemplated to make a

[1] Lehmann, Verh. d. Berl. Anthropol. Ges., 1896, p. 325. On Tiglathpileser's route cf. Toffteen, Researches in Assyrian Geography, p. 11 f.

rebellion of his own. And since it would be dangerous for his prestige to allow this challenge to pass unnoticed, Tiglathpileser immediately marched [1] on to Kinalia, the capital of Unqi. He captured it, carried off its inhabitants into captivity, and made the state an Assyrian province. It was a master stroke, for with the 'Amq in his power Tiglathpileser gained a strong hold upon Syria and from this center was able to strike swiftly at any point, and especially against Hamath and Sam'al. The act did not fail to make an impression. With Unqi the last Hittite state in the heart of Syria was overthrown. That to the last it was relatively free of Aramaean elements appears from the fact that Tiglathpileser in 738 settled 600 Aramaeans of the tribe Damûnu and city of Amlate and 5400 from the city of Dûr in Unqi in the cities Kunalia, Ḫuzarra, Tae, Tarmanazi, Kulmadara, Ḫatatirra, and Sagillu.[2] (Ann. 143. f.). This implies that the inhabitants of the land are not Aramaeans, for it would have been contrary to reason to deport a people to a region where they find others of the same stock (S A 58).

In 739 the Assyrian monarch marched to the north into Urartu and took possession of the region of Ulluba as a vantage point for future campaigns. Perhaps he intended to invade the Urartaean kingdom at this time, but if so he was recalled to Syria by an important rebellion. Whether it was instigated by Sarduris' intrigues, or whether the new province of Unqi was a thorn in the flesh of its neighbors and thus roused them to a revolt, is not quite clear. The main figure in the uprising was Azriyâu of Yaudi or Sam'al, who has nothing to do with the contemporaneous Azariah of Judah with whom he was long confused (A O F I 1 f.). Azriyâu, it seems,

[1] A O F I 9 f. assumes that this took place in 738 with the Azriyâu troubles. That is not impossible. We have preferred, however, to abide by the order given in the Annals.

[2] Identification of most of these towns seems possible. Thus Ḫuzarra may be Ḥazre, Tae may be Kefr Tai (not identical with the Taiâ of Shalm. Mon. col. II. 11), Tomkins, Bab. Or. Rec., III, 6. On the sites cf. Sachau. But Tarmanazi is more probably Armenāz, east of the northern end of the Ǧebel il 'Alā, than Turmanīn (P S B A 27:45). Sagillu is probably the Serǧille on the route Bâra-Marra N.E. of Apamea (Z A XII 43 f.).

usurped the throne of Sam'al (cf. Ch. XIV) and succeeded in gaining the help of the "nineteen districts of Hamath."

Tiglathpileser did not give Hamath time to unite its forces with those of Azriyâu, but from Til-Barsip marched toward Killiz and struck swiftly at the heart of the rebellion in Sam'al. Unfortunately the Annals are very fragmentary at this point, and give us little information as to the scene of the battle. This much, however, we may glean from them: a mountain stronghold is stormed (108–10), whereupon the foe, now reënforced by the arrival of allies, establishes himself in an almost inaccessible place which he fortifies still further by a trench and wall and other means of defense (111–19). The fate of Azriyâu remains doubtful, but since the Assyrian would scarcely relate an unsuccessful siege in such detail, we may assume that Azriyâu met his doom. In his capital, which does not seem to be identical with this stronghold, the Assyrian builds a palace and lays a tribute on the people (123–4). A new king of the royal family, Panammu I (cf. Ch. XIV) seems to have been placed on the throne at this time. We are led to believe that Azriyâu's capital was the city of Kullanî, whose capture the Eponym list records as the great event of 738. Perhaps the real capital of the land, Senğirli, was not in his possession. The site of Kullanî,[1] which is also the Calneh or Calno of Amos 6:2, is probably preserved in the ruins of Kullanhou, about six miles east of Tell Erfâd (Tomkins P S B A '83:61). The fighting then between Azriyâu and Tiglathpileser must have occurred in the mountains in the vicinity of Killiz, or along the upper Afrīn, at the border of Sam'al. After the overthrow of Azriyâu, and the annexation of the district of Kullanī,[2] Tiglathpileser occupied the nineteen districts of Hamath.

[1] The letter A B L no. 372, reporting the sending of Kusaean horses, mentions together Dâna (doubtless the Dānā west of Aleppo), Kullanī, Arpad and Isana. (Tell Isân S.W. of Bireğik P S B A 82: 117) K. 122 A B L, no. 43 refers to Raṣappa, Kullania, Arpad and Isana, whose prefects have neglected to pay their contribution to the temple of the god Ashur. Kullanī's nearness to Arpad is thus certain.

[2] Ann. 125 Kul . . . may represent Kullanī, but this city cannot have been counted among the provinces of Hamath, since it lay in Ya'di.

In these districts of Hamath practically all of that state except the vicinity of the capital itself is contained. It is difficult to understand how these districts can have made common cause with Azriyâu. For between Yaudi and Hamath lay the region of Unqi. It is very strange that this principality is not mentioned in this connection. If Winckler's hypothesis that the subjection of Unqi really took place in 738 be correct, then we would gain a more reasonable picture of the happenings in Hamath. We would then be able to assume that Azriyâu, perhaps as the tool of the Vannic king, organized a great rebellion in which Tutammu of Unqi participated; and since the king of Hamath, Eniel, was loyal to Assyria, the nineteen districts revolted against him and joined the league of Azriyâu. The latter seems to be the quasi king of the nineteen districts. For no other leader appears, and no serious fighting takes place after the capture of Kullanī. The large territory of Hamath seems to fall into the lap of the Assyrian as the fruit of his victory further north.

The nineteen districts are described in Annals 126–133. First come four Phoenician coast cities: (1) Usnu, which seems to be preserved in Qal'at-il-Ḥusn (D P 277) though Tomkins (*l.c.*, 4) compares Ouzoun Dagh, mentioned by the explorer Rey. (2) Siannu, to which is compared Syn, the name of a hamlet near the Nahr Arqa, while Tomkins finds it in il-Ouzanieh, southwest of Ṣahyūn, east of Laodicea. (3) Ṣimirra, to-day Ṣumra in the latitude of Ḥoms. (4) (Rash)-pu-na (Textb. 29). If the reading be correct, the classical Theuprosopon (Ras-ish-Shaq'ā) might be compared. From Rashpuna he occupies all the towns as far as Mt. Saui, a mountain which borders on the Lebanon. Then he names the Mt. Ba'li-ṣapuna, extending as far as Mt. Ammana, home of the ukarinnu wood. Summing this up he says (5) "Sau in its entirety." The term Sau must then include the whole district from Rashpuna to the Ammana (the Antilebanon). The mountain of Saui in the Lesser Inscription I is brought into relation with Ḫatarika: "From Ḫatarika to the mountain of Saua." This mountain I would therefore identify with the Ǧebel Sāyiḥ west of Ḥoms, which slopes down to the Lebanon. Ba'liṣapuna may be the Ǧebel Akkār or Ǧ. Akrūn, both of which are near the Antilebanon. (6) The city of Kar-Hadad. As the next district shows, the sequence is now northerly. We may assume then that Kar-Hadad was at a point between the Antilebanon and Ḥoms — perhaps it was another name of Kadesh or Riblah. (7) Ḫatarika lay, as we have seen, near Arethusa, north of Ḥoms. From here the list jumps over the district of Hamath, which remained true to its king Eniel and mentions (8) Nuqudīna. The latter was a pastoral district, as the name "the shepherds" implies. Perhaps it should be localized at Tarutia [1] (Tarutīn it Tuǧǧār between Ḥamā and Aleppo). (9) The mountain of Ḫasu: This I find in the southern part of the Ǧebel Rīḥā, where there still is a town of Ḥās west of Ma'arrat in No'mān. (10) Ara and the surrounding cities. This is doubtless the classical Arra at Ma'arrat-in-No'mān south of the Ǧebel Rīḥā. (11) The mountain of Sharbua may be found with Tomkins (*l. c.* 5) at Tell Shrēb, east of Arra. (12) The city of Ashḫani — correctly equated by Tomkins with Sheiḥūn east of Apamea. (13) Yadibi — for which Tomkins suggested the site of Ḥatab northwest of Ḥamā, which seems rather far south, however. (14) The mountain of Yaraqu in its entirety, i.e. the Ǧebel Qoṣeir (cf. Ch. VIII). (15) The city of ——. (16) The city Ellitarbi brilliantly identified by Sachau with Il-Athārib, west of Aleppo (S B A '92:337). (17) Zitânu as far as the city of Atinni. Zitânu is no doubt the present Zētān, southwest of Aleppo on the Quwēq river (Tomkins p. 5). Atinni or Adinnu is probably Tell Dānīt near Idlib (cf. Ch. IX). (18) The city of ——. (19) The city of Bumami (unknown). This list makes up the nineteen districts. All that was left of Hamath when they are subtracted was the city itself, the Orontes valley as far as Apamea in the north and in the south to a point above Arethusa and then the Bargylus plateau in the west. The entire nineteen districts were made

[1] I suspect that Tarutia contains an Aramaic word from the root r'ā, "to feed," "pasture"; cf. the form tar'īthā. The connection with "shepherds" is then permissible, since the locality of Tarutia fits excellently into the geographical sequence.

Assyrian provinces and placed under Assyrian administration. 30,300 of the inhabitants were deported to a different portion of the empire and 1223 were settled in distant Ulluba (132–133). Later on, part of these nineteen districts, if not the whole, were included in the province of Ṣimirra, of which Shalmaneser, the son of the Assyrian monarch, was made governor. (A O F II 3.)

The overthrow of Azriyâu's rebellion made a profound impression throughout Syria. All hope of help from Urartu vanished. The princes of the various states appeared with their tribute — Kustaspi of Kummuḫ, Rezin of Damascus, Menahem of Samaria, Hiram of Tyre, Sipittibi'l of Byblos, Urikki of Que, Pisiris of Carchemish, Eniel of Hamath, Panammu of Sam'al, 'Tarḫulara of Gurgum, Sulumal of Melid, several kings from still more northerly regions, and finally Zabibî, queen of Arabia.

After this great success, Tiglathpileser reverted again to his northern campaigns. In 737 he struck at the Medes, in 736 he went to Nal (Naïri), both campaigns being preliminary strategic maneuvers in his plans against the Haldians. In 735 finally he invaded Urartu and besieged the capital Tuspa on the shores of lake Van. He occupied and destroyed the city; but Sarduris with his garrison held the almost impregnable citadel against every attack, and the Assyrians finally had to retreat as winter came on. Nevertheless Tiglathpileser had temporarily broken the influence of the Vannic kings, and was now able to turn his attention to Syria and Palestine once more.

CHAPTER XIII

THE LAST DAYS OF DAMASCUS

As we have remarked, Benhadad III probably perished in the battle of Hadrach in the time of Zakir of Hamath, and was succeeded by Ṭâb-'el.[1] According to Tiglathpileser (ann. 205) Ṭâb-'el came from Bīt-Ḫadāra. Consequently he cannot have been a scion of the dynasty of Hazael, but must have been a usurper. He is referred to in Is. 7: 6 as the father of Rezin (A T U 74). During his reign quiet seems to have prevailed in central Syria. The only events of moment must have occurred in connection with the Ḫatarikka campaigns of 765 and 755. The strength of Israel and of Hamath evidently led Ṭâb-'el to live a peaceful life. Concerning his decease and the time of Rezin's accession we know nothing.

The brief period of glory enjoyed by Israel under Jeroboam II was soon over. The dynasty of Jehu, founded on murder, ends with the murder of Zachariah, son of Jeroboam, after a reign of six months by the ursurper Shallum ben Jabesh (2 Kings 15: 13–16). The murderer himself only enjoys the possession of the throne for a month, when he is attacked in Samaria by Menahem ben Gadi and loses his life (15:17–22). The conditions of civil war accompanying these changes greatly weakened Israel (cf. Is. 9:19, 20). It is peculiarly significant that both Shallum and Menahem are from the region of Gilead, the land which Aram had "threshed" and which had been the scene of so many bloody struggles. They were doubtless hostile to the Aramaeans and were bent on in-

[1] Duhm, Jesaias-ad. 7:6, corrects the name into Ṭôb'el. But I would point out that the name appears to occur in A B L IV no. 221 Ob. 2 as Ṭab-ili, a scribe in Syria, who reports that he has been at Nineveh and has seen the face of Nabu and of the king. He tells also that Abi-ili, the tax overseer of Arpad, is on his way to the prefect. According to A T V 174 the name Tâb'el means "God is wise."

augurating an anti-Aramaean policy. To this end indeed Menahem coveted the aid of Ashur, the bitterest enemy of Aram, while the opposition sought the protection of Egypt. Perhaps with a view to dampening the Egyptian leanings of Israel, Tiglathpileser after subjecting the nineteen districts of Hamath, in 738, dispatched an expedition to Samaria. Indeed the suspicion may be entertained (cf. 2 Kings 15: 19) that Menahem summoned Tiglathpileser to undertake this step in order to strengthen his tottering throne (G V J II 471, 469). But for such aid he had to pay dearly with tribute, which he raised by assessing the citizen-army fifty shekels per head (2 Kings 15: 20). Since 1000 talents are paid and since a talent is composed of 3000 shekels, the strength of Israel's host must have amounted to 60,000 men. The summoning of the king of Assyria is severely condemned by Hosea (5:13, 8: 9).

Menahem died soon after this event, and his son Pekahiah, after a two years' reign, was murdered by his adjutant Pekah ben Remaliah (2 Kings 15: 22 f.). Inasmuch as we subsequently find Pekah allied with Aram, it is reasonable to suppose that his act was dictated by a pro-Aramaean party in Israel. There were many in Israel who realized that only a strong Damascus could prevent the Assyrians from conquering all of Syria. These men desired to join Damascus in common antagonism to Ashur. For this reason Menahem's son, the vassal of Ashur, had to be deposed. And indeed Pekah succeeds in forming a coalition with Aram, Tyre, and Sidon, and Samsî, queen of the Arabs.

This coalition, however, was not yet sufficiently powerful. For an effective resistance against Assyria it was necessary to gain the help of the other Phoenician cities, and of Palestinian states — Ammon, Moab, Judah, Edom Philistaea. The task was urgent and had to be completed before Tiglathpileser concluded his campaigns against Urartu (737–735). Philistaea and Edom seem to have submitted under pressure, but Judah remained obstinate. For this reason Rezin and Pekah moved to attack it, and thereby caused the outbreak of the Syrian-Ephraimite war, for which the prophecy of Isaiah is our chief source of knowledge. (G V J II 473 ff.).

The course of events was one that brought panic to the southern kingdom. "The king's heart and that of his nation trembled like the trees in the forest before the wind" (Is. 7:2). For like a swarm of locusts, "Aram has alighted upon Ephraim." In a terrible battle Pekah has destroyed the Jewish army in the north, and Rezin has taken the harbor of Elath, Israel's seaport on the gulf of Akabah in the south. Pekah hopes to complete the subjugation of Jerusalem alone, but, when unsuccessful, is joined by the army of Rezin. They plan to make the son of Ṭâb-'el, Rezin, king over Judah (Is. 7: 6). In this moment of dire extremity Ahaz of Judah receives the counsel of the prophet Isaiah not to despair before these two smoking torch-butts, Rezin and the son of Remaliah, but to trust in God. Both Aram and Ephraim are "burnt out," their day is over. By divine grace Rezin rules Aram and Pekah Ephraim, but neither shall rule Jerusalem.

Ahaz, however, scorns the advice of Isaiah, and his decision is of momentous character. He summons the help of Tiglathpileser (2 Kings 16: 7, 8) and thereby inaugurates the series of events which lead to the downfall of both Israel and Judah. While the Assyrian did not act immediately, nevertheless the Kings of Damascus and Samaria withdrew from the contemplated siege of Jerusalem. Both probably realized that it was now imperative to prepare for the Assyrian onset, and, since they had crippled Judah effectively, they were, at least, safe from attack in the rear.

In 734 Tiglathpileser, in answer to the petition of Ahaz, undertook a campaign to Philistaea. This powerful stroke was of a masterly character, for it aimed to split the confederacy and to isolate Damascus. Doubtless leaving a strong army and his loyal vassal Eniel of Hamath in guard of his communications in the province of Ṣimirra and to threaten Damascus, Tiglathpileser marched into northern Israel. At this time he took from Israel the cities in Naphtali and Dan (2 Kings 15: 29). His own inscriptions leave us in doubt as to this campaign. The summary in the lesser Inscription I (Textb. 34) says that he took the city "Gal . . . (Gilead?) and the city of Abilakka [1] which is at the entrance of Beth-Omri and the wide . . . li (Naphtali?) and added them to the territory of Assyria." These first blows at Israel, however, merely were intended to lay open the road to the coastal plain. His goal was the Philistine city of Gaza. Here, no doubt, he could affect a junction most quickly with Ahaz of Judah, and furthermore with Gaza he held possession of a point from which he could threaten both Arabia and Egypt. That Egypt was assisting the anti-Assyrian league may be guessed from the fact that king Ḫanun of Gaza fled thither at the advance of Tiglathpileser. After capturing Gaza the Assyrian returned to Beth-Omri and began the deportation of its northern inhabitants.

The events of 733 center chiefly about Damascus, and therefore the name of this city appears again in the Eponym list. After Israel had been punished by the loss of its northern provinces, Tiglathpileser proceeded directly against Damascus (Ann. 195–209). Rezin (Raṣunnu) meets him in battle, trusting in the ancient fortune of Aramaean weapons which had thwarted the Assyrian so many times in the past. But the force of Tiglathpileser's onset breaks his battle array, many of his men and officers are captured, and the latter the captor impales to be a spectacle of horror in the land. Rezin himself takes flight, "like an antelope the gate of his city he entered." The city is now besieged and Rezin is confined in it as a "caged bird." His countless parks around Damascus, the pride of this city in all ages, are destroyed in utter vandalism, so that not one is left. (Bît)-Ḫadāra,[2] the home of Rezin, was besieged and captured and 800 of its inhabitants with their herds and property deported. Similarly 750 prominent citizens were deported from Kuruṣṣa,[3] 550 from Metuna, and a

[1] Usually identified with Abel-beth-Maacaḥ. Textb. 34 interprets, "Abel in the territory of Akko."

[2] This place I would identify with the Adarin of the Tabula Peutingeriana, south of Yabrūd, near the Ḥoms-Damascus highway.

[3] This must be the classical Geroda, today Gerūd, east of Adarin (E K XVII 1473). Perhaps it was the home of Sâsi (above p. 72).

lost number from Irma, towns east of Damascus. Tiglathpileser boasts also that he destroyed 591 towns in the sixteen districts of Damascus like, making them ruin mounds.

In connection with these operations Tiglathpileser recounts an expedition against Samsî, queen of the Arabian tribe of Bir'a who had "transgressed the oath by Shamash" (Ann. 210 f R T P XXXIV f.). Since she was the ally of Damascus, it was necessary to prevent her from bringing aid to Rezin. Tiglathpileser's expeditionary force must have followed the old pilgrim's highway that leads via el-Öla to Mecca. Apparently Samsî was already on the way to Damascus, for at the advance of the Assyrians, she retreated and attempted to lure the enemy farther and farther into the desert. At length, however, she was forced to give battle, and after heavy losses, especially in livestock (30,000 camels and 20,000 cattle), she bowed down before the victor. Owing to this success a number of other Arabian cities and tribes paid homage; the cities — Mas'a, Tema,[1] Ḫayappa, Badana, Ḫatti, and the tribes Saba and Idibail. An Arabian Sheikh Idibi'l was made the guardian of Assyrian interests in Muṣri (i.e. Egypt in Asia — the Sinaitic peninsula) having his seat at Philistaea. From here Tiglathpileser, through his representative, exercised supremacy over the Arabians, since he controlled the outlet of their avenues of commerce, and forced them to pay regular tribute (Ann. 221 f.).

In the meantime a rebellion took place in Samaria. Pekah was murdered and a usurper, Hosea ben Ela, became King in his stead (Annals 228, Less. Inscr. I 17, 2 Kings 15:30). It is not discernible whether differences of attitude toward foreign matters were at the bottom of this event. Tiglathpileser took advantage of the momentary chaos in Israel and marched against Ausi (Hosea); for the Annals, in the paragraph on Beth-Omri (227-234)

[1] This is, no doubt, the Teima north of El-Öla, whence the Aramaic Inscriptions discovered by Doughty and Huber have come (cf. C I S II 113–115). They date from the 5–4 century. The most important and largest is that which records the introduction of the cult of the god Ṣalm of Hagam, and the installation of his priest Ṣalmshēzeb bar Potosiri, whose income is to consist of the fruit of 21 palm trees.

which is unfortunately fragmentary, after mentioning the deposition of Pekah, immediately deal with an attack against Israelitish districts.[1] In the Hebrew version (2 Kings. 17:3) Shalmaneser appears as the king who marched against Hosea. Both accounts may be reconciled if we assume that the later king of Assyria, who then was governor of the province of Ṣimirra, was entrusted by his father with the expedition. About this time Isaiah must have prophesied 8:4. Hosea, frightened by the Assyrian advance, submitted and paid a tribute of 10 talents of gold and 1000 (?) talents of silver. He remained in possession of the kingship by his suzerain's grace (Lesser Inscr. I, 18).

This fresh resistance of Israel seems to have been made in conjunction with similar developments in Philistaea and Phoenicia. Mitinti of Ashkelon, who had apparently submitted in 734, transgressed against his agreement, in the hope that Rezin would be victorious. The defeat of Rezin drove him insane. His son Rukibtu succeeded him. After the Hebrew king Hosea had submitted, Tiglathpileser marched against Ashkelon. Rukibtu, who pleaded with him, was spared, but the Assyrian entered the city and gave fifteen towns of Ashkelon to the trusty Idibi'l of Aribi (Ann. 235 f.). Against Metuna, king of Tyre, he dispatched his Rabshaqeh, or commander-in-chief, and at the latter's approach Tyre also deserted Damascus and paid tribute. Thus Damascus was now completely isolated; its only helpers were intimidated, its fate was sealed. With despairing heart Rezin may have heard the news that the last hope of relief was gone. He was doomed to fight alone against the greatest military power of the world, and in a lost cause. The day that Tiglathpileser hammered against the gates of Damascus marked the end of that city's dream of empire.

Of the great siege we know little, for not even Tiglathpileser's

[1] He carries off 655 prisoners from Bît . . . , others from a city of (Ak?) ba-ra-a (cf. the Talmudic 'Akbara, Neubauer, Geographie, 228 f.), others from Hinaton = Ginnaea (cf. Buhl, Geogr. Pal., p. 82), 550 prisoners from Kana (?) (in Galilee), 400 from -at-bite, 650 from Ir. . . . The cities Aruma and Marum are likewise mentioned. Cf. Buhl, 220, 234.

description of it is extant. Only the fact that Panammu of Sam'al, one of the Syrian tributaries, fought and fell before Damascus (cf. Ch. XIV) gives us an insight into the bitterness of the struggle. In 732, finally, the city was taken, and the kingdom became a province. Rezin was executed (2 Kings 16:9), doubtless in the barbarous manner customary among the ancient Semites. With the fall of Damascus Tighlathpileser was master of Syria, and did not find it necessary to return thither again.

Perhaps with a certain feeling for the dramatic Ahaz (Yauḫazi) of Judah appeared before Tiglathpileser at Damascus (2 Kings 16:10 ff.). It had been long since a king of the Hebrews crossed the threshold of Aram. For centuries they had suffered at the hands of this great and cruel foe. Perhaps Ahaz dreamed that he was treading in David's footsteps, in the dawn of a new and glorious day. Here at Damascus he saw an (Assyrian) altar, and sent a model of it to the priest Uriah at Jerusalem, who constructed a similar one to replace the altar of Solomon.[1] By this act of servility he hoped to please his lord Tiglathpileser.

[1] Cf. Kittel, Studien zur Hebräischen Archäologie, p. 50 ff.

CHAPTER XIV

KINGS OF SAM'AL

In the explorations conducted by F. von Luschan at Senğirli, several other native inscriptions were discovered which give us a welcome and valuable insight into the conditions in northern Syria during the eighth century. A number of additional Kings of the state of Sam'al, not alluded to by the Assyrians, arise again from the grave before our eyes. We have already heard of Gabbar, Ḫaiâ and Kilammu. The next king of whom we now learn the name is Qaral. We only know of him because he is mentioned by his royal son. His name is an indication of his non-Semitic origin, for it seems to be identical with the Aegean "Korulos" (Halévy).[1] Whether he was a son of Kilammu or even his immediate successor we cannot say. It is possible that there is no link missing at all.

Panammu I, son of Qaral, has left us an inscription on a huge, statue of the god Hadad. It was found in 1890 on the mound of Ğerğin, a large Tell south of Senğirli (A Ṡ 47, 45), and is now in the Berlin Museum.[2] It is a votive inscription of 34 lines, the decipherment of which is made difficult by the numerous lacunae caused by the exposure of some 2600 years.

Piously Panammu begins by telling us how divine aid preserved his throne: "I am P., son of Qaral, King of Ya'di, who erected this statue to Hadad lord of the waters (?). There stood by me the divinities Hadad and El and Reshef and Rekabel and Shamash and there gave into my hand Hadad and El and Rekabel and Shamash and Reshef the scepter of blessing (?). And Reshef stood by me and whatever I took in (my) hand . . . that pros-

[1] QRL could be interpreted as qār-ili, "wall of God," but such a formation is unlikely.

[2] Published by Sachau, A S, 1 f. Further elucidated by Müller in the Vienna Oriental Journal, VII, 33 f. and 113 f. Cf. also N S I, p. 159 f.

pered." (1–4.) It deserves attention that the author singles out the war God Reshef for especial mention. He must therefore, have carried on a few successful warlike ventures in spite of his otherwise peaceful vent.

Like Kilammu, the chief interest of Panammu lies in the happiness and prosperity of his people. But he differs from his ancestor in that he is more religious. Childlike is his avowal. "And whatever I ask of the gods they give me" (4). He is indeed a favorite son of the heavenly ones. Among the things which the gods have granted he enumerates "a peaceful life," "great crops of barley, wheat and garlic." Everybody "tilled the land and the vineyard" and thus followed peaceful pursuits (5–7).

The strict logic which marks the thinking of Kilammu is not characteristic of Panammu. For after this description of the blessedness of his reign, he reverts again to its beginning, and superfluously repeats that Hadad gave him the sceptre of blessing (?) when he came to the throne (8–9). "Sword and slander (were cut off) from my father's house" (9), he adds, referring perhaps to early troubles connected with his accession. Again he paints us for the prosperity of his rule, "In my day moreover Ya'di ate and drank. And in my day[1] . . . a man helped (?) his neighbor. And Hadad and El and Rekabel and Shamash and Araq-reshef gave increase and gave me greatness and a sure convenant they made with me" (9–11). But this divine aid is due to a large extent to the efforts of Panammu in behalf of the divine cults on the principle "do ut des." He says "And in my days fat-offering was given to the gods and surely they accepted it from my hands. And so whatever I ask from the gods they surely give abundantly to me and are willing" (12–13). The choice offerings of which he was the donor inclined the tender hearts of the gods toward mercy. And at the command of Hadad he performed building operations: "And I built indeed and raised up this stele of Hadad and the 'place' of Panammu son of Qaral king of Ya'di with the stele of Hadad" (14–15). Briefly the king of

[1] The tenth line is totally obscure.

Ya'di has given us a resumé of the happenings of his reign. His religious disposition, coupled perhaps with an age no longer youthful, cause him to think of the long rest in the grave and of the land of no return, where his spirit will soon be wandering. Every sacrifice or libation at the tombs of the fathers brings food to their languishing spirits and cheers for a little their awful gloom. And the dread that impious descendants might forget this duty causes him to shudder. He dwells at length, therefore, on the theme of the obligations of his descendants toward himself and his god Hadad.

"Whoever of my sons shall hold the sceptre and sit upon my throne and shall strengthen the power, and shall sacrifice . . . to Hadad, and remember the name of Hadad, or who shall say 'May the soul of Panammu eat with thee and may the soul of Panammu drink with thee,' (who) still shall remember the soul of Panammu along with Hadad . . . this his sacrifice . . . may he (the god) look favorably upon it." (15–18.) But if the son that follows him does not fulfill this wish, then may Hadad "not look favorably upon his sacrifice, and whatsoever he shall pray for, may Hadad not grant it; and may Hadad pour out wrath upon him . . . suffer him not to eat because of wrath and withhold sleep from him by night" (22–24). The remaining lines are not clearly understood. They apparently picture tumultuous conditions brought about by the curse which will rest upon those who disregard or desecrate this memorial of Panammu.

A second great Aramaic inscription was found 1888 in the graveyard of Taḫtaly Bunar, whither it seems to have been carried at some occasion from Ğerğīn (A S 48) or possibly from Senğirli itself. It belongs to a memorial statue for Panammu II, erected perhaps upon his grave by his son, "This statue Bar-Rekab set for his father, for Panammu son of Bar-Ṣur, King of Ya'di", it begins. Bar-Ṣur must have been the successor of Panammu I, son of Qaral, though his reign cannot have been of long duration. The fact that his son again bears the name of Panammu is an indication that the line of descent is unbroken. The Inscription may be divided into three parts. The first tells of a revolution in Ya'di, the second relates the accession of Panammu, and the third the death of Panammu and the accession of Bar-Rekab.

Piously Bar-Rekab remarks of his father that "the gods of Ya'di rescued him from his destruction. There was a conspiracy in his father's house" (2). The fragmentary text does not tell us who the main conspirator was, but we can fortunately supply his name with certainty from the inscriptions of Tiglathpileser; he is none other than Azriyâu of Yaudi. We have already seen how, under the leadership of this individual, and possibly with the help of the Haldians, a rebellion of some magnitude took place against Assyrian suzerainty. Evidently the loyal Bar-Ṣur was less fortunate than Eniel of Hamath, who at least remained alive, for Bar-Rekab says that the usurper "brought about destruction in the house of his father and slaughtered his father Bar-Ṣur and murdered 70 kinsmen of his father" (3). Many others loyal to the dynasty were probably put to death "and with the rest thereof indeed (?) he filled the prisons, and made the desolate cities more numerous than the inhabited cities" (4). Panammu, however, escaped the holocaust. The conditions of anarchy in Ya'di brought about a serious increase in the cost of living. "There perished . . . grain and corn and wheat and barley and a Peres (a half measure of wheat) stood at a Shekel and a Shatrab of (barley) stood at a shekel and an Esnab of oil stood at a shekel" (5–6). cf. 2 Kings 7:1.

The second part of the inscription begins: "And my father brought (present) to the king of Ashur and he made him ruler over his father's house and he slew the stone of destruction from his father's house" (7) cf. Is. 8:14. No doubt he refers here to the fate of Azriyâu. Thereupon Panammu seems to have given the king of Ashur a tribute from the treasure of the gods of Ya'di. Then "he opened the prisons and released the prisoners of Ya'di. And my father arose and released the women . . ." (8). The nobility that had been jailed and their harems confined were now liberated as Panammu assumed the reins of government. Immediately after his accession peace and prosperity are restored. (He reëstablished) "his father's house and made it better than it was before; and wheat and barley and grain and corn were abundant in his days (9)." And "cheapness (?) of price" returned again in consequence. "And in the days of my father Panammu he installed cupbearers (?)[1] and charioteers," thus elaborating the pomp of the royal court which before must have been somewhat primitive. "And my father Panammu was made to sit in the midst of powerful kings"[2] (10) but he did not allow himself to be seduced by any one "whether possessor of silver or possessor of gold in his wisdom and righteousness."[3] On the contrary "he grasped the hem of the skirt of his lord the king of Ashur" (11) and the latter placed him over the "governors and princes of Ya'di." The Assyrian prefects even, who had been instituted by Tiglathpileser, as well as the local chieftains, were subordinated to his authority. Indeed he was so loyal that his son can say, "And his lord the king of Assyria gave him preference over the powerful kings" (12). He proved his faithfulness to the great monarch by accompanying him on many a warlike venture. "At the chariot-wheel of his lord Tiglathpileser, king of Ashur, in the campaigns he ran, from the rising sun to the setting sun and . . . in the four quarters of the world." Apparently the vassals, who were less reliable when it came to fighting than the Assyrian troops, were employed to carry out the deportation of the inhabitants of conquered districts, for we learn of Panammu that "the daughter of the east he brought to the west and the daughter of the west he brought to the east" (13–14). As a reward for his distinguished services the Assyrian increased Panammu's territory at the expense of his northern neighbor: "And his lord Tiglathpileser, the king of Ashur (extended) his border through cities from the border

[1] Perhaps derived from Assyrian "kapru," "cup."

[2] Some translate "kings of Kebar" here and in l. 12. This could only be the equivalent of Kibir nâri (or kibir tâmti) and be used here in the sense of the later Eberhannahar, i.e., the region west of the Euphrates.

[3] The trend of thought is doubtful. Possibly he means to say that he made his people possessors of gold and silver.

of Gurgum" (15). This act must have caused resentment in Gurgum and may have brought on the later troubles with Gurgum in Sargon's day (cf. Ch. XV).

The last part of the inscription tells us how Panammu perished. He participated in the siege of Damascus and there his fate overtook him. "Moreover my father Panammu died in camp while following his lord Tiglathpileser, king of Ashur . . . and his kinsfolk bewailed the kingship and the whole camp of the king of Assyria bewailed him; and his lord the king of Ashur took . . . his corpse and instituted for it a lamentation on the way, and brought my father over from Damascus to (this), place" (16–18). Whether or not Panammu died in battle during the many assaults against the walls of Damascus is left untold. His faithfulness to his beloved king of Ashur was thus crowned by a glorious death in his cause.

Bar-Rekab closes by telling us how he himself came to the throne "And as for me, Bar-Rekab, son of Panammu (for the righteous)ness of my father and for my own righteousness, my lord caused me to sit (instead) of my father Panammu, son of Bar-Ṣur" (19–20). The character of this inscription is then finally avowed by its author. "And a memorial this is! So may Hadad and El and Rekabel, my patron, and Shamash and all the gods of Yadi be my (witnesses) before Gods and before men" (22–23).

The third important inscription of this period was found in Sengirli in 1891. It is a building inscription of twenty lines and is preserved perfectly. On the left of the inscription is the figure of its author, Bar-Rekab, in relief, holding in his hand a lotus flower. On the upper part of the stone appear the same symbols that we have already found upon the Kilammu monument, with the addition only of a five-pointed star enclosed in a circle with double contures. (A S 377 f. Pl. LXVII.) The inscription reads as follows:

"I am Bar-Rekab, son of Panammu, king of Sam'al, servant of Tigalthpileser, the lord of the four quarters of the world. For the righteousness of my father and for my own righteousness, my lord Rekabel and my lord Tiglathpileser caused me to sit upon the throne of my father. My father's house labored more than all. And I ran at the wheel of my lord the king of Ashur, in the midst of mighty kings, possessors of silver, possessors of gold. And I took possession of the house of my father and made it better than the house of any one of the mighty kings. And my fellow-kings envied everything. How beautiful is my house! A good house my fathers, the kings of Sam'al did not have. They only had yonder house of Kilammu. And that was their winter-home as well as their summer-home. Therefore I built this house."

A further sculpture representing Bar-Rekab was found at Senğirli. The king is shown in a sitting posture, with a eunuch holding a fan, behind him and in front of him a man whose right hand is uplifted as though he were giving his oath, while under the left arm he is carrying a book, the covers of which are bound in almost modern fashion, and the left hand holds a writing apparatus of Egyptian style with a box for the pens. He must therefore be a scribe or court official. On the right of the king's crown we have the brief inscription: "I am Bar-Rekab, son of Panammu." Still further to the right we read: "My lord Ba'al Harran." The stone must therefore be dedicated to this divinity (A S 347).

The Building-Inscription finds an excellent commentary in the excavations of Senğirli. For here the castle of the kings of Sam'al was unearthed. To emphasize the peculiar architecture of the castle, Koldewey has adopted for it the word Ḫilâni. Thus Sargon states that he built a vestibule, in the manner of a palace of the Hittite country which in the language of Amurri is called Bît-Ḫilâni, in front of the gorgeous gates at Dûr-Sharrukîn (cf. Display Inscr. 161–2, etc.). The excavator believes that in Senğirli we have such a typical Bît-Ḫilâni (A S 189); and, indeed, I am inclined to accept this in view of the hall-building of Bar-Rekab, which seems to have the character of a vestibule like that of Sargon. There are three distinct palaces from different epochs at Senğirli which are designated as Ḫilâni I–III, and for the sake of convenience we will retain this term.

The oldest of these structures is the mighty Ḫilâni I, which stood on the highest point of the city. It is a citadel with two bold towers which overlook the surrounding country for a great distance. Four strongly fortified gates, with huge stone lions guarding the entrance, led into the interior of the castle. Within the court a grave with the sculptured image of a woman — perhaps a favored queen of Sam'al — was found. The interior of the palace is unpretentious, suited only to very modest requirements (A S 175).

The progress in the standard of living in the course of time made this castle insufficient for the needs of a royal family, and so Ḫilâni II was constructed below it. It is a more spacious building but far less powerful than the upper citadel. In the midst of this lower castle, in a niche-like chamber adjoining the main saloon, stood the statue of a God striding upon a postament of horses. In the main room the throne of the kings of Sam'al must have stood.

Ḫilâni III represents the supreme height of Sam'al's glory (A S 167). It is a very large palace, with numerous buildings, suited to the pomp of a great royal court. All the clan and bodyguard of the king had room to dwell here. The faithfulness of Panammu II and Bar-Rekab to the king of Assyria was amply rewarded by a great increase in wealth and prosperity. For only such conditions can account for such a sudden bloom. But all this glory of the new Sam'al seems to have taken an untimely end, for an immense conflagration destroyed the palace, apparently during the lifetime of Bar-Rekab (A S 240). Whether this king rebelled against Sargon under the influence of Midas of Phrygia or Rusash the Haldian, or whether these enemies of Ashur wreaked their vengeance upon his unfortunate city, is a matter of doubt. The former possibility would become a certainty if the passage of the Nimrūd inscription (18) which mentions the subjection along with Hamath of "Yaudu, whose location is afar," refers to our

Ya'di or Sam'al. If so, then Bar-Rekab must have participated in the uprising of Yaubi'di. There was placed in Ḫilâni III an Assyrian stele, perhaps of Tiglathpileser IV, whose inscription was entirely effaced by the flames (A S 27 f.). Sam'al evidently became a province about the end of the seventh century, for in the Assyrian Eponym list, a governor of Sam'al appears in the year 681.

Ḫilâni II and III are connected by a hallway of colonnades. In the campaign of 1904 the northwestern corner of the castle-hill behind this only partly excavated hallway was investigated. In the northern part of the hallway the Bar-Rekab inscription had already been discovered in 1894. Now two other buildings described by the excavators as J and K were unearthed, and in the former the monument of Kilammu was found. As Lidzbarski has seen, J certainly originated at the time of Kilammu; in K it received an extension, perhaps under the same king, and the whole together was called "the house of Kilammu." Since the columned porches of J and K faced south and west, they must have been uncomfortable during the hot season. Therefore Bar-Rekab built an especial summer house in the great northern Hall, which must have been a very pleasant place in the summer days (E S E III 218 f.).

The city of Sam'al was surrounded by fortifications and the ground plan of the whole is ovular in shape. This is quite rare and exceptional among the ancient cities, for the square or rectangular form was the ordinary one. It may be that this oval type is of Hittite origin — the more feasible since Senğirli is in reality a creation of the Hittite era. Two other great Hittite cities, the mounds of Carchemish (Ğerabis) and Kadesh (Qal'at el Mudīq) show the very same characteristics (A S 178 f.). The ancient Hittite engineers realized that all angles are a weakness in defense. Three complete walls entirely girded the city and two other walls partly surrounded it. Along the outer wall were more than 100 towers (A S 174). These walls were of great strength. Furthermore, the three gateways that led through these walls, being by nature the most vulnerable points, were enormously fortified. The besieger of Sam'al had to break through five of such gates before he reached the citadel. And then he faced the task of attacking Ḫilâni I with its immense walls — five yards in thickness — and its towers which were seventeen yards square at the base. To the architect of antiquity the fortress of Sam'al must indeed have seemed impregnable (A S 182). But all this greatness crumpled before the terrible impact of the Assyrian onset. It must instil into us a great admiration for the army that could storm this city. So great was the catastrophe for Sam'al that for fifty years it must have lain quite desolate. It was not until the time of Essarhaddon that another small castle was built on the ruins of Ḫilâni I, probably as a home for the Assyrian garrison and the governor (A S 242). Here stood a stele of Essarhaddon with an Assyrian inscription in which he speaks of his wars with the Egyptians. (A S 36.) The sculpture represents the monarch and two conquered kings, Tirhaqa the Egyptian, and Ba'al of Tyre. This palace was apparently destroyed ca. 300 B.C., at the time when the Acropolis of Iṣlaḥḫiye was founded on the site of the later Nicopolis of Pompey which usurped the place and importance of Sam'al. (A S 177.)

There is one point of which we still must make mention. What is the relation of the Ya'di to Sam'al? Winckler (A O F I 18) and later also Schiffer (S A 94) have had recourse to complicated arguments to show that they are two different states adjoining each other, and forming at times a dual monarchy. But this seems rather unsatisfactory.[1] Both Panammu I and Panammu II are called King of Ya'di in the two inscriptions from Ğerğīn, but Bar-Rekab speaks of his fathers as the "Kings of Sam'al" and in the same breath calls himself King of Ya'di. Kilammu also is king of Ya'di. The Assyrians speak of Ḫaiā and Panammu as

[1] The city of Kullanī appears as capital of Yaudi under Azriyâu, and in 864 a governor of this city is mentioned. But since the portion of Sam'al which had held to Azriyâu became a province immediately, it is but natural that it should remain an especial administrative district in later days.

kings of Sam'al, but of Azriyau as being Yaudi. We may suppose then that Ya'di was the name of the city Senğirli while Sam'al was the name of the larger kingdom, or else we can hold with Lidzbarski that both terms are identical, the former being merely the Hittite and the latter the Semitic name of the state.

CHAPTER XV

THE LAST REBELLIONS

Tiglathpileser was succeeded by his son Shalmaneser IV (727–722), the former governor of the province of Ṣimirra. The only principalities which now still preserved at least a shadow of independence were the (greatly reduced) kingdoms of Hamath, Carchemish, Sam'al, and Gurgum. On the Phoenician coast the Tyrian state seems to have caused a little trouble, as must be concluded from the treaty of Essarhaddon with Ba'al of Tyre.[1] Perhaps this state intended to make common cause with its ancient ally Israel. For the latter, under its foolish king Hoshea, was deluded by Sewe of Egypt (alias Sib'u of Muṣri) into a revolt against the Assyrians (2 Kings 17:1–6). The king of Ashur then laid siege to Samaria and captured it. The Old Testament account tacitly assumes that Shalmaneser is the conquerer of Samaria. With this the claims of Sargon conflict. Thus he asserts in his Annals (11–17) that the fall of Samaria and the battle of Dur-ilu took place in his first year (721). But here he must be in error; for the Babylonian chronicle (I 33) and also K 1349, a text dating from the second year of Sargon, place the Babylonian troubles in 720 (Olmstead 43 f.). It would seem then that Olmstead is correct when he argues that the siege of Samaria began in 725 and ended in 723 during the lifetime of Shalmaneser (A J S L '05, 179 ff.). It would indeed be difficult to imagine how Samaria, if destroyed by Sargon in 721, could participate in the rebellion of 720. On the other hand it is highly probable that a change of rulers in Ashur should encourage Israel to a new revolt. Sargon's claims may then apply to the renewed suppression of Samaria in 720 and it is probable that the deportation of 27,290 people from this city

[1] A O F II, p. 10.

(Ann. 15) is identical with that referred to in 2 Kings 17:6 and took place at this time. Indeed it seems to me that in 2 Kings 17:5 the first capture of Samaria has been lost in our text, for it must have been told there that Shalmaneser captured the rebellious city before he could cast Hoshea into prison. The second capture under Sargon then led to the removal of the population to Mesopotamia and Media (on the regions cf. Olmstead 71 f.) and the colonization of the city with people "from all lands" (Ann. 16).

During his first year Sargon was probably busy establishing his authority in Assyria. Then in his second year he was forced to turn to Babylonia and to fight at Durilu with Humbanigash of Elam and Merodach-Baladan. It seems that his reverse at Dur-ilu was due to the fact that he was already engaged in the campaigns in Syria, which took place in the same year. For the Syrian realm was threatened by a new uprising. It had been instigated chiefly by the Egyptians and had two main centers — Philistaea and Hamath. Ḫanun of Gaza, who had fled to Egypt in 734, had returned to his kingdom after Tiglathpileser's death. The Arabian tribes were now confronted by the same conditions as previously and so they abandoned their allegiance to Ashur. The Assyrian governor Idib'il of Aribi either yielded and made common cause with the others or else was put out of the way. The Ambassadors of Philistaea also tried to draw Judah into the rebellion, but failed, since Isaiah opposed them (14:32 G V J 489). In the north Hamath, under a certain Yaubi'di,[1] succeeded in stirring up the Assyrian provinces Arpad, Ṣimirra, Damascus, Samaria, and probably Sam'al. It might be assumed that the two movements in Philistaea and Hamath were entirely independent of one another, but it seems to me that the Display inscription wishes intentionally to correlate the two, when, contrary to the chronology, it places the struggle with Ḫanun before that with Azriyâu. The purpose of this must be to introduce Sib'u of Muṣri as the leading

[1] The name seems to contain "Yahweh," "Yau has removed my curse (?)." The alternate form Ilubidi, as Olmstead, 48, suggests, is simply (M. ilu) Yaubidi with the Ya dropped and the god-sign "ilu" drawn into the name.

figure in the events of this year. True, Haldian influence may also have been exercised at Hamath (Olmstead 48).

Sargon followed the fundamental principle of Assyrian strategy and struck swiftly at his foes before they were able to complete their preparations. After crossing the Euphrates he marched straight for the territory of Hamath. Yaubi'di, a rustic (ṣab-ḫubshi), who had no right to the kingship, a "Hittite,"[1] sought to secure the throne upon which the faithful Eniel had sat so long. Whether he ever did rule in Hamath is doubtful, for Display 33 and Nimrûd 8 appear to contradict each other. His fortress is Qarqar, "his beloved city" (i.e. his birthplace?). Here in the glorious days of Irḫuleni the Assyrians had been thwarted. Perhaps Yaubi'di believed that he could bring back those times once more. But if so he did not expedite his preparations sufficiently. For like a whirlwind Sargon was upon him. Qarqar was besieged, stormed, and sacked. The hapless Yaubi'di with his family and warriors was brought in chains to Assyria and later flayed alive. Hamath itself was also captured (2 Kings 18:34, Olmstead 179). According to Display 33 Sargon visited all the rebellious districts and killed the revolutionists. Hamath henceforth became a province under Assyrian administrators. 6300 loyal Assyrians were settled there. A military levy of 300 chariots (Display 35 only 200) and 600 horsemen was made upon Hamath. (Stele I 57f.) Daiukku of Man (Deioces the Mede: Herodotus I 16) with his clan was later deported to the district of Hamath, according to Display 49.

From northern Israel, after visiting no doubt Damascus and Samaria, Sargon advanced to meet Ḫanun of Gaza and Sib'u of Muṣri.[2] Ḫanun did not make the mistake of attempting to hold

[1] Ethnically he was an Aramaean, as his name proves. "Hittite" is the type of an excitable, faithless person, just as "Gutaean" is the type of a brutal and rough individual; cf. Texb. 38.

[2] G V J II 485 makes Sewe — Sib'u another name for Pi'anchi (cf. B A R IV '08 § 812 f.). Equally possible is the assumption that Sib'u is merely the commander of Pi'anchi's armies. In regard to the Arabian Muṣri (Winckler, M V A G '98, 1) we must be very skeptical; cf. Olmstead, 56 ff.; G V J II 488 f. This Muṣri must not be confounded with that in Cilicia.

Gaza alone, but retired and united with the appoaching Egyptian reënforcements to the south at Rapiḫu (Tell Refaḥ). Here a great battle with Sargon was fought, ending in an Assyrian victory. Sib'u fled alone, "like a shepherd whose sheep have been robbed" (Annals 29), before the weapons of Sargon and utterly disappeared (Display 26). Ḫanun was captured and brought to Ashur in chains, with 9033 of his people and their possessions (Ann. 30 f.). Rapiḫu was destroyed, but Gaza was apparently spared, for it was too valuable for the Assyrian to destroy it unnecessarily.

New trouble in Syria arose for Sargon several years later at Carchemish.[1] This state, through the skillful diplomacy of its rulers, had remained independent, while all its neighbors were ground under Ashur's foot. It was the last bulwark of Hittite civilization in that latitude. Doubtless it too had a chiefly Aramaean population, but the superior culture and intelligence of the old inhabitants gave it its character and governed its policies. The state of Carchemish always participated in the Syrian rebellions and yet always managed to withdraw its neck from the noose before it was too late. Its policy was to take no risks; for Carchemish was a great commercial city and commercial interests must militate against any interruption of prosperity. Now, however, Carchemish was completely isolated, for its western neighbor, Sam'al, had also become an Assyrian province. Its king, Pisiris, must have realized that Ashur would very soon annex Carchemish, if only for the sake of its treasures. Furthermore, a new figure had loomed up upon the theater of history — Mita of Muski or Midas of Phrygia (A O F II 136) — who promised to renew the ancient empire of the Hittites. Already his legions were pouring into Que and Armenia. What was more natural than that the ruler of Carchemish should hope for deliverance through him? In 717 Pisiris sent an appeal to Midas for assistance against Ashur.

[1] On this city cf. Hogarth, Carchemish, 1914; Proceedings of Brit. Acad., V, "Hittite Problems and the Excavations at Carchemish"; also King, History of Babylon, 1915, p. 127 f.

The uprising of Carchemish was no light matter for Sargon. If Midas offered effective aid, then renewed rebellions from the Amanus to Philistaea could be expected. The road to the sea would be blocked and Mesopotamia laid open to invasion. Again, however, the great speed of his attack thwarted his foes. Before Midas could move to help Pisiris, Sargon was hammering at the gates of Carchemish. We know nothing of the siege. It seems that Pisiris did not hold out to the bitter end, for no holocaust of death came over the city. Sargon merely states that he led Pisiris and his family and all the conspirators with their property away to Assyria. From the treasure-house he took 11 Talents of bright gold, 2100 Talents of silver, 10 Talents of bronze. Of other booty he mentions elephant hides and tusks, as well as weapons. The troops of the city, 50 chariots, 200 horsemen, 3000 (Annals 50 gives 300) infantry, he attached to his own legions (XIV 1 42 f.). The military strength of the city was evidently not so very great. If Carchemish suffered from the siege we do not know, but bricks bearing Sargon's name have been found there. The fall of Carchemish was celebrated as a great event. In its honor the earliest document of Sargon's reign — the Nimrûd inscription — was erected in the palace of the monarch where his treasure was deposited and especially the great booty of Carchemish which his hand had won (l. 21 f). That Carchemish still retained its commercial importance is vouched for by the fact that the Mina of Carchemish was used alongside of the regular royal Mina of the Assyrians down to the time of the fall of Nineveh (A D D II 268).

During the next years Sargon took up the struggle with the Haldians under Rusash. The details of this struggle do not concern us here; suffice it to say that he utterly smashed the Vannic state. Rusash ended his life with suicide in 714.[1] After expeditions to Media and Asia Minor we find Sargon again concerned with Syria in 711. The northernmost Syrian state, Gurgum,

[1] Recently a new and valuable text relating to the Armenian campaign of 714 has been published by Thureau-Dangin, Une Relation de la Huitième Campagne de Sargon, '12.

caused him trouble. Its king Tarḫulara was murdered by his own son Mutallu,[1] doubtless because he refused to side with the Phrygian Midas against Assyria. Sargon, with his bodyguard, hastened to the capital of Gurgum, Marqasi (Marʿash)and captured Mutallu with the whole clan of Bît-Pa'alla [2] and their spoil. He made Gurgum a province, and redistributed the land among the inhabitants (Display 83–89). Sargon must have been in Syria at this time — perhaps engaged in the Philistaean campaign against Azuri of Ashdod — else he could not have struck so swiftly at Mutallu. Whether the Mutallu of Kummuḫ who made common cause with Argistis of Urartu in 708 and whose land became an Assyrian province is to be identified with Mutallu of Gurgum (Winckler, Sargon XLI) is uncertain. If this were so the previous news of Mutallu's capture must have been "greatly exaggerated." But perhaps the identity in names is merely a coincidence.

All of Syria, in so far as it was Aramaean or even bastard-Aramaean, had now come under the sway of Assyria. True, the Phoenician cities on the coastal rim, protected by the mountain barriers, still retained their autonomy for some time during the next century. But Phoenicia, while of great importance in the development of civilization, stands with its face toward the setting sun. It thus lies apart from the great movements which mark the course of Oriental history. Aram, however, stood with Israel in the path of progress, and, heroically resisting, was ground beneath the chariot wheels.

But just in this its tragic fate Aram, like Israel, was led to the consummation of its mission. It is indeed a spectacle almost without analogy that the conquered can force its language upon the conqueror and upon a vast territory like the fertile crescent from Egypt to the Persian Gulf. True the Amorites of old had accepted the speech of the Akkadians, but here the Akkadians

[1] Variants of an inaccurate nature make Tarḫulara directly deposed by Sargon XIV 10 Pavé des portes, IV, 28.

[2] Doubtless the home of Tarḫulara (Winckler, Sargon, XXX). The name is clearly Aramaic.

were vastly superior in culture. The Aramaeans, however, were inferior in this respect to their conquerors. How then could such an anomaly come to pass? Undoubtedly the policy of the Assyrian kings of deporting captive Aramaeans in such large numbers into the immediate vicinity of Nineveh, together with the complete absorption of Babylonia by new arrivals from the Neğd, was to a large extent instrumental in the overthrow of the Assyrian as the spoken language of the common people. But with this also is coupled the fact that the Aramaeans were great merchants, and that they were especially numerous in the region of the great trade routes of Syria, Mesopotamia, and Chaldaea. Thus their language had the opportunity of becoming a medium of exchange. And its greater simplicity of structure, coupled with an easy and convenient script, gave it an inestimable advantage over its only possible competitor, the Assyrian. Furthermore, the destruction of the Aramaic states separated this language from all national aspirations or religious propaganda, so that no prejudice against its use could arise. After the fall of Nineveh (606) nothing could hinder its triumphal march. It became the necessary means of communication between Iranian east and the Semitic west. It succeeded eventually in entirely displacing the Hebrew and Canaanitic; even in Tyre and Sidon the old mother-tongue perished, and in Edom and North Arabia as well. From the Persian gulf to Cilicia, and from Edessa to Petra and to Syene on the Nile the Aramaic became the language of the common people. And it maintained its supremacy even against the inroads of Hellenistic civilization until finally the great onset of Islam brought its rule to a sudden end.

But withal, its importance for the world was then consummated. It had been the language of Christ and his apostles, and of the early Christian Church especially in the Osroëne. Without it the expansion of Christianity in the Orient would have been unthinkable, just as it would have been unthinkable in the Occident without the Greek. This then is the historical debt which the world owes the Aramaeans.

INDEX OF BIBLE PASSAGES

INDEX OF BIBLE PASSAGES

INDEX OF GEOGRAPHICAL NAMES

INDEX OF GEOGRAPHICAL NAMES

GENERAL INDEX

www.ingramcontent.com/pod-product-compliance
Lightning Source LLC
LaVergne TN
LVHW050646100826
845148LV00011B/2009